Emily's Story

The Brave Journey of an Orphan Train Rider

Clark Kidder

Second Edition: First Printing

© 2007 and 2013 by Clark Kidder

All rights reserved. International copyright secured. No part of this book may be reproduced, stored in a retrieval system, or transmitted in any form or by any means—electronic, mechanical, photocopying, recording, or otherwise—without the prior written permission of the author, except for the inclusion of brief quotations in an acknowledged review.

Library of Congress Control Number: 2007905288
ISBN 13: 978-0-615-15313-1

Cover design by Kari Bryant

Back cover photo: Orphan train on the Atchinson, Topeka, & Santa Fe Railroad line, location and date unknown (Santa Fe Collection, Kansas State Historical Society. Used with permission.)

Printed by Gorham Printing
Centralia, Washington

Dedication

*In loving memory of my paternal grandparents,
Earl and Emily Kidder.
Thank you for enriching my life with laughter, love,
and precious memories.
Sweet dreams.*

*To Becki —
Pleasant Journeys —
Clark Kidder*

Contents

Dedication iii

Contents v

Acknowledgments vii

Introduction ix

Chapter One—Children In Need 1

Chapter Two—Brace Founds The Children's Aid Society 7

Chapter Three—Emily Loses Her Home 23

Chapter Four—Emily Rides the Orphan Train 41

Chapter Five—A Romance Blossoms 83

Chapter Six—A Place to Call Home 105

Chapter Seven—Reunions and Farewells 113

Chapter Eight—A Final Home for Emily 129

Appendix I (The Rest of The Story) 139

Appendix II (Endnotes) 153

Appendix III (Sources For Records) 161

Appendix IV (Bibliography) 167

Appendix V (Teacher's Guide) 171

Appendix VI (Resources Available From Author) 179

The Children 181

About the Author 183

Acknowledgments

This book would not have been possible without the help of many people and organizations. Many thanks to the late Victor Remer and daughter, Alice, of the Children's Aid Society. Victor once served as Executive Director of the Children's Aid Society. He and Alice managed the archives there while I was compiling this book. Thank you, Mary Ellen Johnson, and the Orphan Train Heritage Society of America. Mary Ellen founded the Orphan Train Heritage Society of America, and has always been of so much help to me. Your efforts on behalf of all orphan train riders are to be commended. Thank you, Mr. and Mrs. Charles Rose for so graciously allowing me to excerpt Mamie Gunderson's memories of life in the Home for Destitute Children, giving us a rare glimpse at what life was like in an orphanage just after the turn of the Twentieth Century.

The author is also very grateful to the following people and organizations for assistance with photographs and information: the Adams County Historical Society; the New York Historical Society; the Museum of the City of New York; the New York State Library; Corbis; the Chicago Historical Society; the Milton Historical Society; the Library of Congress; the Kansas State Historical Society; Northern Illinois University/Regional History Center; the University of Akron Library; Mrs. Walter Sayre for allowing me access to Reverend H. D. Clarke's scrapbooks, and Carol Arnold for editorial assistance. Many thanks to Ellen J. Froelich, George

Elwood, and Leon Yost. Many thanks to Phil Paone for assistance with historical research and documents, Robert Parmelee for information on the Parmelee Bus Company of Chicago, Micaela Sullivan-Fowler at the Middleton (WI) Health Sciences Library, Greg Highby, PhD at the American Institute of the History of Pharmacy, John Knight for information on his mother, Gertrude (Bell) Knight, Jennifer Bohrnstedt and Donna Nordmark for manuscript critique, Joseph S. Dalton for his help with information on Reverend Charles J. Roberts, Joan M. Drahos for providing information on her father Alfred Bauman; Dorothy Gunn for history and photos of the United Brethren (now Mt. Zion Methodist) Church of Janesville, Wisconsin, and last, but certainly not least, the Reese and Kidder families.

Introduction

In each of our lives there are a handful of very special people who inevitably have a tremendous impact on us. For me, two such people were my paternal grandparents, Earl and Emily Kidder.

Many children never really get to know their grandparents, but I had the good fortune of having mine reside in an apartment on the west side of our Wisconsin farmhouse. The farm consisted of nearly 175 acres, and was located in Milton Township, in the north-central part of Rock County.

I wasn't much more than five years old when I decided I wanted to sleep in my grandparents' apartment. The two apartments were attached and shared two common doors, much like a duplex. I would spend most of the next eighteen years of my life with them, sharing meals, listening to their wonderful stories of yesteryear, and soaking up every bit of love they could spare. Grandma Emily would often shoo me over to my parents' side of the house, telling me that I needed to spend more time with them. I could never understand why she had been so emphatic about it. My answer would be found many years later, and as you read this book, the answer will become apparent to you as well.

In 1981, at age eighteen, I followed a suggestion made by my aunt, Mildred (Kidder) Yahnke, that I should begin researching our family tree. I decided to do just that and began interviewing my paternal grandparents and other family members. By then, Grandpa Earl was eighty-eight and

Grandma Emily was eighty-nine. The stories they told about our ancestors fascinated me, but I was particularly interested in the story of how they met, and what their young lives were like.

Grandma told me that she was an orphan and was placed in an orphanage in Brooklyn, New York when she was about eight years old. She told me her parents died of pneumonia and that her brother Richard was also placed in the orphanage, but was later adopted. She recalled how a minister by the last name of Clarke had brought her to the Midwest on a train under the auspices of the Children's Aid Society of New York City.

I took note of everything at the time, but I concentrated my efforts on tracing the Kidder family tree, as the Kidders had settled in the area some 130 years previous, and there was a wealth of records and information to be had in the immediate area. In addition, many of my Kidder relatives still resided in the area.

It was not until several years after my grandparents passed away that I read about an organization called The Orphan Train Heritage Society of America, which gathered and disseminated information on Orphan Train riders. It occurred to me that my grandmother, Emily, may have been one of the children that were sent West on what they were now calling "Orphan Trains."

I later learned that a woman in my hometown of Milton had several volumes of journals and scrapbooks kept by a minister named Herman D. Clarke. She mentioned to my aunt Mildred that her mother Emily's name was in the journals. My aunt informed me of this and I made a call to the lady that had the journals. As it turned out, Reverend Clarke was the minister that my grandmother often referred to as having brought her out on the train from New York, for in his journals was a wedding picture of my grandparents and a history of grandma's trip on the orphan train. The woman that had them was the widow of Reverend Clarke's grandson.

I contacted the Children's Aid Society in New York and they confirmed that they were still in possession of a file on my grandmother, and that she was one of some 2,750 children that they sent to Wisconsin by 1910. What followed was a journey of discovery.

Reading the reports that Reverend Clarke sent to the Society regarding my grandmother was difficult at times, but also very interesting. I found it hard to comprehend in this day and age with all the bureaucracy and red tape involved when one wants to adopt a child or become a foster parent, that there was a time in America's not so distant past that groups of children were offered to anyone that happened to express an interest in them. Many orphan train riders described the process as not unlike going to pick out a puppy. With just two weeks' notice, the citizenry of an entire town and its surrounding countryside was invited to come and take their pick out of a group of homeless children.

How very fortunate I was that Reverend Clarke's journals survived. I felt that it was important to publish them in some form, so as to preserve them for future generations and I began a search for the six volumes that he created—one for each of his grandchildren, and one for his adopted daughter, Emma. Six of the seven journals were located, all of which contained slightly different information. My book was subsequently published in 2001 by Heritage Books, Incorporated of Bowie, Maryland, and was titled *Orphan Trains and Their Precious Cargo—The Life's Work of Reverend H. D. Clarke*.

Reverend Clarke placed over 1,200 children in homes from the orphan trains. The stories he recorded in his journals about their trials and triumphs were absolutely incredible. I came to realize that the plight of children then was not so different than what it is today—there are still many thousands of children around the world that are in need of a real home, the tender touch of someone who loves them, and the sense of place that comes from that. Many people still feel that it is preferable to bring a child up in a home in the country versus one in the city, but as Reverend Clarke so aptly points out in his journals, no matter what the setting, the main ingredient in bringing a child up properly is LOVE.

It doesn't seem possible that over two decades have passed since I lost my grandparents. As I look back upon those precious years spent with them, I realize, unequivocally, they were the best years of my life. I miss them both so very much.

The majority of the stories of the individual orphan train riders are nearly forgotten now in the attic of American history. This book is my attempt to rescue my grandmother's story from such a fate. Hers is a story of triumph over personal tragedy and seemingly insurmountable odds. The results of my years of research are presented in the pages that follow, revealing the unspoken chapters in my grandmother's incredible life. It is my hope that this book will inspire those that are still fortunate enough to have a grandparent living to do their very best to cultivate a close relationship with them.

Respectfully,

Clark Kidder
Janesville, Wisconsin
March 26, 2006

In saving "your child,"
"our children,"
we are saving ourselves also.

—Meigs V. Crouse, Superintendent of
The Children's Home of Cincinnati, 1893.

Chapter One

Children in Need

"Common domestic animals are usually more humanely provided for than the paupers in some of these institutions."

—New York State Commission

A real crisis began to unfold on the streets of New York City in the late 1840s. The crisis involved children, and lots of them. Immigrants were pouring into New York at the rate of 1,000 per day, primarily from Germany and Ireland.[1] Abandoned babies were being found in the streets at the rate of one every day. They would often be left on doorsteps, in vestibules, even in trash cans and vacant lots. For those still alive, the only refuge was the almshouse. Few survived there.

At the time that the city's population was about 500,000 the police estimated that there were 10,000 boys and girls living on the streets.[2] In 1849, New York City's chief of police, George Matsell, decided to sound an alarm about the "constantly increasing number of vagrant, idle and vicious children of both sexes, who infest our public thoroughfares, hotels and docks." His report estimated that 3,000 children were living on the streets of Manhattan.[3] As such, his numbers were far more conservative than those of social reformers, who commonly put the number of vagrant children at 10,000, and sometimes even 30,000 or 40,000.

A short time later, New Yorkers were horrified by a grand jury report on serious crimes:

"Of the higher grades of felony, four-fifths of the complaints examined have been against minors. And two-thirds of all complaints acted on during the term have been against persons between the ages of 19 and 21."[4]

Traditionally, such children were taken in and cared for by friends, neighbors, and extended family when the parents either died or were unable to care for them. All this changed with the flood of immigrants.

Although orphanages were not unheard of in Colonial America, they were few and far between. By 1850, the sheer numbers of displaced children in New York City, as well as other large Eastern cities, necessitated that officials begin building more and more such institutions to warehouse the children. Such places were known by various names, such as almshouse, workhouse, and poorhouse. These places were far from humane in their treatment of children, and provided appalling living conditions. A New York State commission filed this report in response: "The great mass of poor houses are most disgraceful memorials of the public charity. Common domestic animals are usually more humanely provided for than the paupers in some of these institutions."[5]

Eventually, private orphanages and juvenile asylums were built to house the children as officials began to realize just how inhumane the conditions were in the poorhouses and similar institutions.

During the period following the Civil War the population of the United States grew rapidly, and the problems of juvenile reform became greater and more dynamic. Immigrants from Italy and Eastern Europe, following their Irish and German predecessors, began to dominate New York's cultural landscape.

As the century progressed, these immigrants worked longer hours and lived in increasingly poor conditions. This gave the children more opportunities to

New York City was not alone when it came to the problem of dealing with children in need. A policeman escorted these four destitute siblings to a local Humane Society in Cincinnati, Ohio in 1903. (Children's Home of Cincinnati, Ohio)

get into mischief on the city streets. There was no structure of extended families in place as there was back in the mother country from which the immigrants came. Thousands lived in familial isolation, unable to rely on a grandparent or an aunt or uncle, to help care for the young children.

In 1865 the New York State Legislature enacted a bill to control the "disorderly child." The act provided that, upon complaint of a parent or guardian, a magistrate or justice of the peace could "issue a warrant for the apprehension of the offender." If a child was found to be disorderly the court was required to commit the child to the House of Refuge. Though the Disorderly Child Act hinged on parental complaint, it represented a move away from parental authority. Under the Act, a child did not need to have committed a crime—"disorderly" conduct was sufficient justification for placement.[6]

The law treated kids seven and older as adults—those twelve years and older could be put to death for the crime of stealing.[7] Children were thrust into institutions among adults of every kind, including the diseased, the senile, and the mentally ill.

As late as 1851 there were still 4,000 inmates under twenty-one years old in New York's adult prison, 800 of whom were fourteen or younger, and 176 were less than ten years old.[8]

The problem only worsened with the advent of the industrial age. Thousands of people moved from rural areas into the city to obtain work at one of the many new factories being built. The sheer number of job

Children play among the "stagnant pools of liquid poison, offensive smells, and dirty houses." (Cincinnati Historical Society)

applicants allowed factory owners to pay them a mere pittance for their labor. Labor unions were nonexistent. There was a housing shortage due to the influx of thousands of immigrants that competed with farmers for the factory jobs, allowing landlords to command high rent for places that were barely suitable to live in. Even in cases where the mother, father, and several children were working in the family, there was still not enough money to subsist. Children as young as five or six would often labor long hours in the factories and receive just pennies a day.

When many mothers began to work in factories, they would often leave their children locked in rooms all day, or would leave them free to roam the streets. Some of these children prostituted themselves. Others shined shoes, peddled newspapers, sold matches, ran errands, or picked rags.

By 1890, day nurseries were established throughout the city, but poorer families did not often take advantage of them. These were the days long before Social Security was even heard of. A family's survival depended entirely on the ability of the parents to stay healthy and maintain a steady income. This was especially true of families living in the inner city, without the resources that an extended family may have otherwise provided. Diseases such as tuberculosis, smallpox, yellow fever, typhus, and measles were rampant and easily spread in the overcrowded tenement buildings where several families often shared a single apartment. It was not uncommon for poultry and livestock to inhabit the same quarters as people did.

Chapter Two
Brace Founds The Children's Aid Society

"—all this motley throng of infantile misery and childish guilt passed through our doors, telling their simple stories of suffering, and loneliness, and temptation, until our hearts became sick."

—Charles Loring Brace

Charles Loring Brace was born in 1826 in Litchfield, Connecticut. His parents moved to Hartford when Charles was yet a boy, and that is where Charles would grow up. His family had done well both financially and socially, and came from old New England stock. Brace would be greatly influenced by the sermons of the renowned theologian Horace Bushnell who preached naturalness in regard to child raising, discouraging the use of threats and coercion when shaping a child's character. Bushnell may have also played some role in Brace's decision to join the ministry.[1]

Brace graduated from Yale in 1846, and then attended the Yale Divinity School and the Union Theological Seminary, but after completing his education, he was undecided about joining the church ministry. He was greatly interested in missionary work and soon found himself working as a city missionary at the Five Points Mission in New York City. His work at Five Points would lay the foundation for what would become his own personal mission in the years ensuing.

While on a trip to Europe in 1850, Brace toured England's "ragged" schools, which believed in reforming the children rather than simply incarcerating them—a novel idea at the time. He had undoubtedly learned of the British system of "transportation," which was a well-known practice used as far back as the early 1700s. This system provided for the shipment of the country's less desirable citizens to North America, Capetown, and Australia. Removal from their home country was considered their punishment. By the time Brace appeared on the scene, one other class of people was added to the list of those being shipped off—the poor, particularly women and children, were also being resettled.[2]

In addition to the government, the British Ladies' Female Emigrant Society was also given approval to send more women out of the country. It seems the frontiers of the Empire needed labor, and in some cases prospective wives for the male settlers. Canada became a favorite destination for the relocation of women and children. One group even found its way to the English colony of Wakefield, Kansas in America. Twenty-one boys were sent there in 1869 under the auspices of the London Home and Refuge for Destitute Children.[3]

In 1852, at the age of twenty-five, Brace decided that something needed to be done to alleviate New York City's problem of so many destitute, delinquent, and homeless children. He referred to them as "the dangerous classes."

After touring such places as Blackwell's Island and the Five Points district on the Lower East Side with its overcrowded tenement buildings, he was aghast at the "immense number of boys and girls floating and drifting about our streets, with hardly any assignable home or occupation, who continually swelled the multitude of criminals, prostitutes and vagrants."[4]

In the Foundling Hospital, which was operated by the city, he found that nine out of ten of the illegitimate and abandoned babies had died. "The truth seems to be," Brace observed, "that each infant needs one nurse or caretaker, and that if you place these delicate creatures in large companies together in any public building, an immense proportion are sure to die."[5]

Institutions such as the New York House of Refuge and the New York Juvenile Asylum often housed nearly 500 youngsters, and Brace concluded early on that such conditions were robbing children of the most basic of needs…the love and attention of parents and extended family. In 1857, at the First Convention of Managers and Superintendents of Houses of Refuge and Schools of Reform, which was held in New York City, a then 31 year-old Brace delivered this address:

> "We hear, in these Reports from the Institutions, of one person presiding over five hundred children, and it is asserted that he manages this family on the purest parental principles…I hold that it is impossible for a man to feel towards them in any degree as a father feels towards his own offspring…The poor boy in the great house can never become to us like the child of our flesh and blood; in some degree he must be a stranger; and my observation has been, that where you have large numbers of children together, you cannot have that direct sympathy and interest and personal management which make the family so beneficial to children."[6]

Brace proceeded to write a series of newspaper articles outlining the problem as he saw it. He called for the formation of a new kind of organization to deal with these problems. The organization would be solely devoted to the needs of poor and homeless children. Brace appealed to the public for support of the Aid Society's endeavors: "As Christian men we cannot look upon this great multitude of unhappy, deserted, and degraded boys and girls without feeling our responsibility to God for them."[7]

In March of 1853, the Children's Aid Society of New York City became a reality. A small office was established at the corner of Broadway and Amity Street. Brace served as the secretary and initially agreed to occupy the post for one year for a salary of $1,000.00. He ended up staying until his death in 1890, thirty-seven and a half years later. His two sons, Robert N. and Charles, Jr. later succeeded him. Following in his father's footsteps, Charles, Jr. also served thirty-seven and a half years.

Brace described the reaction of the children to the newly formed Children's Aid Society in one of his books:

> "Most touching of all was the crowd of wandering little ones who immediately found their way to the office. Ragged young girls who had nowhere to lay their heads; children driven from drunkards' homes; orphans who slept where they could find a box or stairway; boys cast out by step-mothers or step-fathers; newsboys, whose incessant answer to our question, 'Where do you live?' rang in our ears—'Don't live nowhere!' Little bootblacks, young peddlers, 'canawl-boys' who seem to drift into the city every winter and live a vagabond life, pickpockets and petty thieves trying to get honest work; child beggars and flower-sellers growing up to enter courses of crime—all this motley throng of infantile misery and childish guilt passed through our doors, telling their simple stories of suffering and loneliness and temptation, until our hearts became sick."[8]

Brace outlined his ideas, as well as the new Society's mission to save the children in question. The Aid Society would build lodging houses, reading rooms, a Boy's Hotel, an Italian mission, cottages on Coney Island, Bath Beach for the "Fresh Air" children, a Farm school for boys, the Elizabeth Home For Girls, and Industrial schools for both boys and girls, where "they were taught the common niceties, and with that, house work and trades."

The Society issued the statement "We hope especially to be the means

*Charles Loring Brace, founder of the Children's Aid Society,
as he appeared in the 1880s.
(Children's Aid Society)*

of draining the city of these children, by communicating with farmers, manufacturers, or families in the country, who may have need of such for employment. When homeless boys are found by our agents, we mean to get them homes in the families of respectable, needy persons in the city, and put them in the way of an honest living."⁹ He continued, "The family is God's Reformatory; and every child of bad habits who can secure a place in a Christian home is in the best possible place for his improvement." Especially in the West, where there were "many spare places at the table of life."

The news spread quickly among the outcast children of the city, many of whom were newsboys who had one lodging house that was devoted solely to them.

The News Boys' Lodging House, founded in 1874 by Charles Loring Brace. (Children's Aid Society)

Reverend H. D. Clarke, a placing agent who worked for the Society for a decade beginning in 1900, later described his interaction with this particular class of waifs in his journals:

> "Occasionally I placed one who had been a newsboy. These boys were what we may call unique—none like them in many ways. They were light-hearted and ready to make light of their own hard lot. Often they had tattered clothes and looks of exposure. They are as merry as a circus clown and as full of powers to imitate them. Their morals are not the best, but often the soul of honor in defending the rights of others less favored.
>
> They borrow of each other, papers and money, and always pay back. They'll decide the last nickel with a suffering neighboring boy. Sleeping in dry goods boxes when bankrupt and eating crusts, they toil on in the strife, tempted to steal and cheat and lie. Some of our great preachers and statesmen have risen from this band of street waif.
>
> The Society has a Lodging House especially for newsboys. I attended a banquet given them by a wealthy merchant, who had once been a newsboy. He gives this on Washington's Birthday annually. No newsgirls were invited. The boys filed in between two policemen. They formed a double row and in between the rows they smuggled in a few girls. They went in, but not to the dining hall. The police pretended not to see them. Coming out from the tables or feast, the boys had something in their pockets for the girls. One, handing some to a waiting girl, said, 'Here's something fur yer sick mudder.'
>
> There were twelve hundred boys in this Home. They had their own orchestra and speeches for prominent men in sympathy with their needs."[10]

Charles Brace expressed his views on placing out as well: "The best of all asylums for the outcast child is the *farmer's home*." Brace's plan became known as "placing out," and the "free home" movement.

*Older siblings were often burdened with the care of younger ones.
New York City, circa 1890. (Corbis)*

By the end of the first year, the Children's Aid Society could report "We have thus far sent off to homes in the country, or to places where they could earn a living, 164 boys and 43 girls, of whom some 20 were taken from prison, where they had been placed for being homeless in the streets."[11]

In September 1854, Brace's dream of sending children to new homes beyond New York's borders to the rural American West became a reality. The Aid Society sent forty-seven boys and girls (mostly boys) aged seven to fifteen to a little town in Michigan called Dowagiac. They departed New York on the steamship *Isaac Newton* with emigrant tickets for Detroit. They were accompanied by an agent for the Aid Society named Rev. Mr. Smith who later recalled the trip:

> "...you can hardly imagine the delight of the children as they looked, many of them for the first time, upon country scenery. Each one must see everything we passed, find its name, and make his

own comments. 'What's that, mister?' 'A cornfield.' 'Oh, yes, them's what makes buckwheaters.' 'Look at them cows (oxen plowing); my mother used to milk cows.' As we whirled through orchards loaded with large, red apples, their enthusiasm rose to the highest pitch. It was difficult to keep them within doors. Arms stretched out, hats swinging, eyes swimming, mouths watering, and all screaming—'oh! oh! just look at 'em! Mister, be they any sich in Michigan? Then I'm in for that place—three cheers for Michigan!' We had been riding in comparative quiet for nearly an hour, when all at once the greatest excitement broke out. We were passing a cornfield spread over with ripe, yellow pumpkins. 'Oh! yonder! look! Just look at 'em!' and in an instant the same exclamation was echoed from forty-seven mouths. 'Jist look at 'em! What a heap of mushmillons!' 'Mister, do they make mushmillons in Michigan?' 'Ah, fellers, aint that the country tho'— won't we have nice things to eat?' 'Yes; and won't we sell some, too?' 'Hip! hip! boys; three cheers for Michigan!'"[12]

Within a week, every boy and girl had a home. Brace wrote, "On the whole, the first experiment of sending children West is a very happy one, and I am sure there are places enough with good families in Michigan, Illinois, Iowa, and Wisconsin, to give every poor boy and girl in New York a permanent home. The only difficulty is to bring the children to the homes."[13] This was the beginning of what is now referred to as the *Orphan Train Era*.

The American Civil War killed nearly a half million men between 1861 and 1865, leaving families without a father to support them. Mothers were forced to give their children up, and many were subsequently rocked by the iron cradle—an orphan train. Many of the children sent on the trains were indeed true orphans, but a great many of them were either half-orphans (with one surviving parent), or had both parents still living, but unable to provide adequate care for them. It was common during those days to refer to half-orphans, or children who had been deserted by their parents, as orphans.

By the 1870s the orphan trains of the Children's Aid Society were rolling into towns in more than thirty states. More than 3,000 children a year were finding new homes in the country. Children born in America made up the majority, followed by immigrant children from Germany and Ireland.[14]

There was no shortage of children needing homes, demonstrated by the fact that in one three-month period in 1874, 90,000 homeless people slept in New York City police stations.[15] The peak year for the Children's Aid Society came in 1875, when a total of 4,026 children, along with a few needy adults, whom the society regularly placed in small numbers, made the journey westward.[16]

Unwashed and barely dressed in ill-fitting, tattered clothing in their "before" photo, the same two brothers – dressed in the first new clothes they ever owned — appear cheerful after a bath and haircut in their "after" photo, and are ready to take a trip on the orphan train. (Scrapbook of Rev. H. D. Clarke)

Other organizations in the East, such as the Catholic-run New York Foundling Home in New York City, and the New England Home for Little Wanderers in Boston, began sending children to western homes, as did charities within the larger Midwestern cities, such as the Children's Aid Society of Indiana, the Children's Home of Cincinnati, and the Children's Home Society of Chicago. Between 1883 and 1909, twenty-eight states set up children's home societies for placing children in families within a state.[17]

Each organization had its own rules regarding placement. For instance, the New York Foundling Hospital, founded in 1869 by Sister Mary Irene of the Sisters of Charity, preferred to locate the foster parents prior to the child being sent out on the train. They would sew the last name of the child's new foster parent in the lapel and pin a piece of paper with a number on the child's chest, which corresponded with the number assigned to the waiting parents. The very day that the Foundling Hospital was opened, a baby was left on the front stoop. Later, a wicker baby basket was placed in the front lobby to receive foundlings anonymously. This organization rarely sent children out over the age of four, and thus the trains that carried their children were often called "baby trains."

One newspaper writer covering the story of a baby train's arrival interviewed a new foster father, who said: "Beats the stork all hollow. We asked for a boy of 18 months with brown hair and blue eyes and the bill was filled to the last specification. The young rascal even has my name tacked on him."[18] By the close of the century the Foundling Hospital reported that they had placed just over 90,000 children in western homes.[19] They would send their last group of orphans on an orphan train in 1923.[20]

In those early days, the *West* was simply the farthest-most point to which the railroad had extended its tracks. The area we now know as the Midwest was often referred to as the "Old Northwest." The great majority of children were placed in Midwestern states such as Indiana, Illinois, Michigan, Iowa, Minnesota, and Wisconsin. Iowa was the state where Brace personally preferred to send children.

The Children's Aid Society conducted a survey in 1900, which concluded that 87% of the children they sent to western homes grew up to become respectable citizens. There were exceptions. Many of the children became mere slaves of those who took them. Some were beaten. A fair number ran away from such homes and would quite often return to New York City. The following article ran in the Beloit (WI) Daily News in 1908, and chronicles one boy's unfortunate experience:

"TAKEN OFF ORPHANS' TRAIN
TO LIFE OF BITTER CRUELTY
—
George Spence, beaten with heavy club,
sent to detention home.

Milwaukee, Nov, 27 — Ten years ago on a cold night in January in Milwaukee, among a trainload of hundreds of orphans sent from New York and shipped about the country in quest of guardians, sat little 3-year-old George Spence.

Spence was the name of his parents of whom all trace has now been lost, but on the orphans' special he was known as No. 17, because that number was sewed on his sleeve.

A few minutes after the train arrived here John Pacala, a laborer, 801 Eleventh Avenue, entered the car and took the child to his home. Young Spence, now 13 years old, appeared in junvenile [sic] court bearing marks of inhuman treatment and Judge Neelen, taking him from Pacala, sent him to the county home for dependent children.

A tale of suffering told by the waif, who was given the name of Alfred Pacala by his self-chosen guardian, was corroborated by Supt. Zachariah Clayton, Wisconsin Humane society. He admitted the theft, but during his confession Judge Neelen noticed his red and swollen ears and his apparent hesitancy in talking as he looked at his guardian.

When Judge Neelen asked what caused his ears to appear so, Mr. Clayton said young Spence had been made to work hard by Pacala, who had frequently lifted him in the air by his ears and held him there for several minutes, and had beaten him with whips and with a sawed off ball club, the top of which was filled with lead. He said the boy's body was a mass of bruises and cuts.

Officials stated that Pacala is the third of the New York orphans who has been sent to the Detention home and taken from guardians because of inhuman treatment."

Of course, such circumstances also existed in New York City. What fate would have awaited them if they had remained in the New York institution, or the streets from which they were taken? It certainly would not have been a favorable one.

Even as late as 1908 it was reported that 90,000 children could not attend school in New York City due to a lack of space.[21] Immigrants continued to flood into America, with some 14 million arriving between 1900 and 1914.[22]

In the Children's Aid Society's Annual Report for 1917, the noteworthy careers of many of the children they previously placed were listed: "A Governor of a State, a Governor of a Territory, two members of congress, two District Attorneys, two Sheriffs, two Mayors, a Justice of the Supreme Court, four Judges, two college professors, a cashier of an insurance company, twenty-four clergymen, seven high school Principals, two School Superintendents, an Auditor-General of a State, nine members of State Legislatures, two artists, a Senate Clerk, six railroad officials, eighteen journalists, thirty-four bankers, nineteen physicians, thirty-five lawyers, four civil engineers, and any number of business and professional men, clerks, mechanics, farmers and their wives, and others who have acquired property and filled positions of honor and trust."

Changes in attitudes and the implementation of new foster care laws eventually brought the orphan train era to an end. Social workers believed that it was more beneficial to allow a child to remain with his or her birth parents and siblings, or with a member of the extended family if at all possible.

A significant change in national policy took place after President Theodore Roosevelt arranged for a White House Conference on Dependent Children in 1909—where modern child welfare would be born. The conference was attended by more than 200 of the most prominent figures in American child welfare and social work, and was held on January 25 and 26. In direct reference to the Children's Aid Societies' policies, a report made following the conference declared:

> "Children of parents of worthy character, suffering from temporary misfortune, and children of reasonable efficient and deserving mothers who are without the support of the normal breadwinner, should as a rule be kept with their parents, such aid being given as may be necessary to maintain suitable homes for the rearing of children."[23]

The report continued with another rejection of Aid Society policy:

> "Such homes should be selected by a most careful process of investigation, carried on by skilled agents through personal investigation and with due regard to the religious faith of the child. After children are placed in homes, adequate visitation with careful consideration of the physical, mental, moral, and spiritual training and development of each child on the part of the responsible home finding agency, is essential."[24]

Many states passed laws that either forbade the placement of orphans within their borders from out of state, or required placement agencies to put up bonds, usually of $1,000, to ensure that the agency immediately remove—in the words of an Iowa bond from 1907—"any child having contagious or incurable disease, or having any deformity or being of feeble mind or of vicious character [or] any child. . . which shall become a public charge within the period of five years."[25] Michigan had been the first, in 1895. The states of Indiana, Illinois, and Minnesota followed suit in 1899, followed by Missouri and Nebraska two years later. By late 1927 there were only five states—Michigan, Kansas, Iowa, Nebraska, and Texas—still allowing the Children's Aid Society to make placements within their borders.[26]

The mass migration of children had surpassed even the great Children's Crusade of the Middle Ages and assured that the orphan trains would forever become a part of America's social history and folklore. The practice of placing out would later prove to be an important step in the evolution of child welfare in America.

It is estimated that around 200,000 children were placed on these orphan trains in the seventy-five year span between 1854 and 1929. Historians believe there are nearly two million descendants of these orphan train riders.

It may be argued that the real story of the orphan train era is not one of institutions and policies, but of the individual children who made those journeys into places unknown—forever changing the landscape of the American West.

One of these remarkable children happened to be this writer's grandmother, Emily (Reese) Kidder.

Chapter Three

Emily Loses Her Home

"The discontinuance of pillows after a trial of over a year has been attended with very beneficial results"

—Annual Report for the Home For Destitute Children, 1900.

Emily Florence Reese entered this world at 5:00 a.m. on Monday, March 28th, 1892 in a little rented apartment above a store located at 1333 Myrtle Avenue in Brooklyn, New York. She was the tenth child born to her parents, Lewis and Laura Amelia (Scott) Reese.[1] Lewis was a shoemaker by trade and was born in New York City. He learned the trade from his father, Moses L. Levy, a Jew who changed his last name from Levy to Reese sometime between 1850 and 1860 to avoid conflict from being identified as having a common Jewish surname. Emily's mother, Laura, was born in Brooklyn, her father was a prominent baker in the Bushwick section. Lewis and Laura were in their early forties by the time Emily arrived.

The names of Emily's older siblings were Clarence, Elizabeth "Jane," Fanny, Jenny "Joan," May, Laura (who died of tuberculosis the year Emily was born), Martin, Lewis, Jr., and Richard.

A severe depression was gripping the nation two years after Emily's birth, and the Reese family, along with so many thousands of others, suffered greatly because of it. Residents of inner cities had an especially hard time of it. Those living in rural areas could at least grow their own food. Jobs became scarce. People could no longer afford new pairs of shoes, and Lewis' business decreased dramatically. He and Laura found it increasingly difficult to feed and clothe their many children.

Because of circumstances still unknown, Lewis abandoned Laura and the children in about 1895. Perhaps he could no longer face the harsh reality that his children were going hungry, and was helpless to do anything about it. Emily was just three years old at the time.

Laura, in her destitution, borrowed forty-five dollars from an acquaintance to pay bills, but when she was unable to pay it back the authorities were notified and she was hauled off to jail. The older children were left alone to care for the younger siblings in Laura's absence. After sitting in jail for several weeks, Laura was able to come to an agreement with the judge to pay the loan back in installments, and she was released.[2]

Birthplace of Emily (Reese) Kidder, 1333 Myrtle Ave., Brooklyn, New York. Notice the overhead tram. Tax Department photo, circa 1940. (NYC Municipal Archives)

One day, a knock on the door would change Emily's life and the lives of her entire family, forever. Authorities from the Brooklyn branch of the Society for the Prevention of Cruelty to Children came calling. They learned that Laura was providing inadequate care for her children. Emily and her brother, Richard, who was two years her senior, were taken into the custody of the Society. The Society did not have facilities for holding children for any length of time, so they began looking for a suitable place to send them. It was decided that they were to become wards of the Home for Destitute Children—Industrial School No. 3, located at 217 Sterling Place, on Park Slope, between Flatbush and Vanderbilt Avenues in Brooklyn.

Richard and Emily were loaded into an enclosed coach, and they made their way towards the Home through the streets of Brooklyn. They had to be wondering if they would ever see their family again.

The Home for Destitute Children and Industrial School No. 3, 217 Sterling Place, Brooklyn, New York, on December 19, 1915. (Brooklyn Eagle/Brooklyn Public Library)

They soon heard the driver summon the horses to stop. As Richard and Emily stepped out of the coach, they found themselves looking up at a rather ominous looking brick structure. Chiseled in stone above the front entrance, which was situated at the top of about a dozen cement steps, was the word "HOME."

The Home was a branch of the Brooklyn Industrial School Association, founded in 1854 by Mrs. Harriet Brown of Williamsburg. By 1900, the Association was operating six such schools throughout Brooklyn. They were numbered one through six, in the order that they were established. The Home on Sterling Place served as the "parent Society."[3]

At the Home on Sterling Place, which Richard and Emily were about to enter, over three hundred young boys and girls were housed together, yet separately.

Richard and Emily made their way up the stairs towards the front door of the Home, with one of the S.P.P.C. officers on either side of them. They made their way through the doors to a nearby office that had the word "Matron" painted on its door. The Matron got them registered, and they were escorted upstairs to the girls' and boys' dorms. Richard and Emily were now in a Home, but not the one they had hoped for.

Richard and Emily are listed as wards of the Home for Destitute Children, 217 Sterling Place, Brooklyn, New York, on the 1900 U.S. Census.

On June 15, 1900, census taker Mary Smith would record Richard and Emily's names among the 327 little souls confined to the Home on Sterling Place. Over 300 of these were public charges. The children ranged from five to twelve years in age.

In the Home's Annual Report for the year 1900, the policies adopted by the administrators of the Home were clearly spelled out, and reveal just how regimented and impersonal life in the Home was for its many young occupants:

- "The discontinuance of pillows after a trial of over a year has been attended with very beneficial results"
- "The first Thursday of the month is the day appointed for the visits of the children's parents and friends, which must take place between the hours of 2 to 4 p.m. and 6 to 8 p.m. It is the earnest request of managers that on visits, parents should not supply the children with cake, candies, and unripe fruits."
- "The epidemic of sore heads in now a thing of the past."

The report further stated:

"Since our Home opened its doors to children who needed a temporary home and kindly care, over 4,436 such children have been received and cared for. We find the causes of dependence of these children to be (1) father or mother in hospital for a brief period; (2) they were living in broken homes, father or mother dead or separated, and (3) they were living in evil surroundings."

Richard and Emily were taken "on trial" by a couple from Brooklyn in 1903, at the ages of thirteen and eleven, respectively. Their names were William and Hannah MacKay. For reasons yet unknown, the MacKays decided they would like to keep Richard, but not Emily. Emily was taken back to the Home after she and Richard exchanged tearful goodbyes. The MacKay's intended to eventually adopt Richard, but they had to adhere to rules of the Home, and to City of Brooklyn law at the time:

> "Children shall not be indentured or adopted in the City of Brooklyn, except under peculiarly favorable circumstances.
>
> "Any person applying for a child will be required to furnish two or more references for investigation. If these prove satisfactory, then an 'agreement for three months' trial' shall be signed by the applicant, and five dollars paid at the time, as an equivalent for clothing provided for the child on going out.
>
> "If, after the expiration of three months, the child proves satisfactory, notice shall be sent to the Indenture Committee, and, with the approval of the Executive Board, an Agreement, to be binding until the child attains the age of 18 years, shall be sent for signature to those who have taken the child; this Agreement bearing date from the time the child first left the 'Home,' to be returned and placed on file at the 'Home'—a duplicate, signed by two of the Official Board, to be sent to the parties taking the child.
>
> "An annual payment of Ten Dollars shall be made by persons taking a child, until he, or she, reaches the age of 16 years, when Twelve Dollars shall be paid till the boy or girl has attained the age of 18 years.
>
> "The money received for the service of the child and placed in the bank, shall be given to the child upon attaining the age of 21 years, and the child, on receiving the money, shall give a receipt for the same, which receipt shall be placed in the safe at the Home."[4]

It was not until 1911, when Richard attained the age of twenty-one, that the MacKays decided to adopt him. This was not unusual, as many families would wait until they were quite certain the child they reared fit in well with the family, and would indeed remain in contact even after reaching legal age.

Emily would later sadly recall that Richard's adoptive parents brought him back to see her just one time during her entire stay at the orphanage.

Indeed, Emily was not to fare near as well as Richard. She would spend nearly six long years of her young life in the confines of the Home.

Despite the fact that some of their siblings were much older, and at least two were married, none of them offered to take either Richard or Emily into their homes. The reason for this remains a mystery, but it would have a long-lasting effect on how Richard and Emily would later view these older siblings.

One of Emily's fellow wards at the Home was a girl named Mamie Gunderson. Mamie was eventually sent west on an orphan train in 1905 and placed in Rock Port, Missouri. Shortly before her death, she recorded some of the experiences she had at the Home in a notebook for her children—many of which were experiences undoubtedly shared by Emily:

Mamie Gunderson, a fellow ward of Emily Reese's at the Home For Destitute Children in Brooklyn, New York. (Charles A. Rose)

"On the front of the building, as you go up the long wide steps, inscribed in large stone letters was 'Industrial Home for Destitute Children.' This orphanage had to be large to house nearly 500 children. It contained a school, chapel, hospital, and wards. The hospital and wards were on the fifth floor, as well as the dormitories. The building was divided into two wings. The center was spacious, which was a part of the nursery, as well as schoolrooms. The first floor was a dining room where both boys and girls ate their meals. The dining room consisted of long narrow tables like our picnic tables. We sat on stools. At each place was a granite cup of milk, and two slices of bread. This was our meal, three times a day, with one exception—on visiting days, we had soup. Also on this floor was the girl's playroom.

The bathroom was a large tub with water pipes overhead, with a long trough where each girl would wash her face and hands, and scrub her head before going in to the dining room each morning. You wonder why I said scrub her head? The girls had their hair cut short with clippers so they could scrub their hair each morning [this was to deter the spread of head lice and ringworm].

On the other wing of the building, on the same floor, was the boy's playroom and washroom. The girls and boys were separated entirely, even on the playground. The playground was all cement with a brick wall all around, and a brick wall to separate the boys from the girls. There were no trees or grass, so for shelter, there was a roof which extended over both the boys and girls playground. Extending all around the playground was a high brick wall. No one could climb in or out.

Between the two wings was the nursery for babies under four years old. They had a veranda to play out on. This extended out from the building. We could see the little ones from the girl's playground while out playing.

The bakery and laundry rooms were all in the basement. I was never in the basement but once, to take a basket of girl's clothes to the laundry. The fourth and fifth floors were mostly all dormitories. The little girls' dormitory was on the fifth floor. There was also a detention room, and hospital. I was in the hospital once when I had the chicken pox. I had the chicken pox so mild I enjoyed being in the ward as we had a nice bed and pillows, and play toys.

Nursery at the Home for Destitute Children, which was reserved for "babies under four years old." "All were so well during the summer that we hoped for a year of continued health; but alas, the ills that children are heir to were lurking in the air, and we did not escape. Although more than half of the children were stricken with mumps or chicken-pox...only one death occurred." (Annual Report of the Home, 1908)

On weekdays, we attended school, and on Sundays, we went outside the building to attend the church of our affiliation. There were numerous churches. The matron went with us.

On Christmas day, the children sang carols for the attendance. On several occasions I remember a group of children went out to the various churches and sang Christmas carols. I was in one of the groups. The church people gave us treats, which were rare in the orphanage.

In the summertime we went to the park [likely Prospect Park—a large park situated a few blocks south of the Home]. Of course, we marched there, and stayed together, and marched back.

Everything we did was by the bell, and everywhere we went we marched in single file. There was a bell for rising in the morning,

One of the dormitories at the Home for Destitute children, circa 1908. The dorms were located on the fourth and fifth floors. (Annual Report of the Home, 1908)

Cobbling Class at the Home for Destitute Children, circa 1908. Some 3,927 pairs of shoes were repaired by the boys in 1907. Boys were typically taught cobbling, and how to cane chairs. Girls were taught sewing, cooking, and basket making. (Annual Report of the Home, 1908)

and a bell to march to the dining room. In the summertime, we also had classes in sewing, and made baskets. The boys learned to cane chairs, and mend shoes. When it was bad weather on Sundays we had Chapel services with the boys and girls together, but were separated, with the boys on one side, and the girls on the other side. It was the same in school.

We had a library in one of the schoolrooms. We could only use it in the evening, but it was only for those children who could read good. I was one who could use the library. The cooking class was very interesting. We could eat what we cooked, which *was* a treat. Otherwise, the only treat we got was on Sunday night, when we had one molasses cookie.

I'll have to tell you about the cookies. When we went to the little girls' dormitory to pull down the covers, there was about four or five of us. We went out in the hall, and heard the dumbwaiter coming up from the kitchen on first floor to the fifth floor, for the hospital. On the dumb waiter was a big pan full of those molasses cookies, a pail of milk, and a pan full of sliced bread. We waited until the girl who was pulling up the dumb waiter shut the door, and was on her way upstairs. We opened up the door, and each girl took a handful of cookies, and ran back into the dormitory, and crawled under the bed and ate them! It was like children raiding the cookie jar, so we didn't see any harm in it.

The playroom was a part of the room where the tubs were for cleaning up in the mornings. There were no chairs, tables, or any other furniture. We sat on the floor. We didn't have any toys. All I had, as I remember, was a doll's trunk, which had been donated by the churches. All the Protestant churches in Brooklyn donated whatever they could, as the orphanage was supported by the churches.

Whenever it was a rainy or cold day, we all sat on the floor, and the caretaker would teach us Bible chapters. She would read a line, and we would repeat it, then another line, and repeat, then the two lines, etc., until we could repeat the whole chapter. When I left the orphanage I knew about ten chapters or more.

In the summertime, we would go to the park and sit on the grass, which was so different from the playground at the orphanage. One time we went to Coney Island where there were all kinds of amusements, such as the Bumpety-Bumps, Shoot to Shoot, and a Merry-Go-Round. The trip was paid for by a man named Harmon. How do I know? We gave a yell, 'Harmon, Harmon, HARMON—Hip, Hip, Hurrah!'

Classroom at the Home for Destitute Children. Note that the boys are separated from the girls. The plaid dresses and the aprons that Mamie Gunderson described are clearly visible on the girls, as is their closely cropped hair.
(Annual Report of the Home, 1908)

The clothes we wore were all alike. The girls wore plaid dresses with just a plain waist and skirt, long sleeves, and an apron of blue and white check was worn over the dress. We made one change, once a week—a clean apron. The boys wore a dark suit with a checked apron over the suit.

The clothes were made in a sewing room by three or four women. The girls had to sweep the sewing room once a week. I'm not sure if they made the boys suits, or only their aprons. The girls who were eight or nine years old were taught how to sew. I think I was eight years old when I learned to sew. We sewed buttons on clothes, hemmed towels, and made buttonholes. We also learned to hemstitch by drawing threads from material, and hemstitching around the border. We used handkerchiefs for this.

We were disciplined so strictly. We couldn't do any talking at any time, only on the playground and in the playroom. One day, as we were looking at our cookbooks in cooking class, following along with the teacher's instructions on a recipe, I missed her say 'add vanilla.' I said to the girl near me, 'What did she say that word was?' The

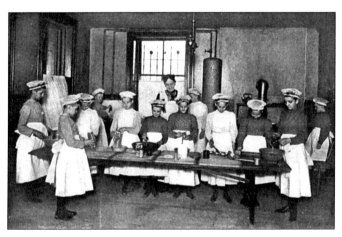

Cooking class at the Home for Destitute Children.
"The cooking classes are taught faithfully and are great blessings to the girls who have had the privilege of taking lessons. They are taught in a practical way to cook plain, simple, wholesome dishes, to be careful in selecting and buying, make the fire, wash dishes, set the table, clean the kitchen, and serve as waitresses. The children are bright and very receptive...when they leave the Home they are better fitted for the battle of life. One little girl, after leaving the Home, wrote that she was cooking her father's meals, her mother being dead."
(Annual Report of the Home, 1908)

teacher heard me talking, and sent me to the Superintendent's office. I had to explain what happened, and she gave me a good scolding. That was all, but I was really scared. I was afraid it would be a real whipping. When I think of such a trivial thing as that, I wonder what a mother would do if her child asked her such a question? It really wasn't the question, but I had broken a rule by talking. That was the real punishment. I never forgot. I was so interested in the recipe that the words just slipped out of my mouth.

We didn't observe many holidays, as I remember. Thanksgiving wasn't thought of, as that is a day of feasting. We didn't have anything special. Christmas was the day we had a special treat. Each child had an apple and orange…no candy, or other luxuries. A Christmas tree

Needy children are fed at the James Center in Manhattan in a program sponsored by the Children's Aid Society. Note their closely cropped hair. A nickel bought them a hot lunch of beef stew, whole wheat bread, potatoes, onions, two glasses of milk and applesauce. However, no child who lacked a nickel was turned away. Before their morning meal, they would say this prayer: "Father, we thank thee for the night, For the blessings of morning light; For rest and food and loving care, And all that makes the world so fair. Amen." Before their noon meal they would pray: "We thank thee for this food, and all thy mercies. Keep us from harm, and make us good children. Amen." (Corbis)

was placed in the chapel with a few decorations, and a few gifts. If the parents didn't come and bring their children a gift, then each child got a gift that was placed under the tree. I remember I got a book on birds. I read that book over and over, until I knew it by heart. My mother didn't come that year. I only remember her coming one time. It was soon after she placed us in the orphanage. A girl who stayed in the reception room off from the office called my name out when I was in the playroom one day. I knew what that meant, so I went up the back stairs, through a long hall. At the end of the long hall, sitting on a bench, was my mother. I ran up to her, and instead of kissing her and looking at her, I laid my head in her lap, and cried. I guess I was

The Elizabeth Home For Girls, 307 E. 12th St., New York, New York. Emily was sent here on November 17, 1905. (Children's Aid Society)

Emily's record from the files of the Children's Aid Society. Information on Emily's parents and family is unfortunately absent. Her year of birth is given as 1903, but should correctly be 1892. Her day of birth is also wrong, as it should be the twenty-eighth of March. Note the approval given for "going to a western home," and the date they Emily departed with Rev. H. D. Clarke. (Children's Aid Society)

overjoyed. I thought she was so beautiful. I never saw her dressed up before. I can't remember the conversation we had, or whether my brothers were there. All I could remember was her sweet face. She brought me a silk handkerchief, which I carry with me to this day.

She wrote me a letter after I left the orphanage. I didn't receive it for several weeks, as no one in the town [in Rock Port, Missouri] knew me, and my letter was put in the dead letter office. By the time I got the letter, my mother had written that she was going to move in two weeks. I wrote her right away. I don't know if she ever got it or not. I never heard from her again."

In 1905, just months after the Children's Aid Society sent Mamie

Gunderson to Rock Port, Missouri on an orphan train, Emily herself became one of their new wards, and was assigned number 3993.41/388.

Apparently Emily became a bit rebellious during her lengthy stay at the Home for Destitute Children, for on Friday, November 17th, 1905, she was sent to the Elizabeth Home For Girls in Manhattan. This Home was operated by the Children's Aid Society and had the dubious distinction of housing those girls deemed "incorrigible." It was located at 307 12th Street, and was built in 1892 in memory of Miss Elizabeth Davenport Wheeler by her family.

The Home had dormitories, classrooms, a lounge and six private rooms with names like Daisy, Pansy and Forget-Me-Not; there were fifty-eight beds in all. It also had a washing and drying room—laundry was an important trade taught to the girls, along with typing and dress-making.[5]

Three hundred and twenty-six girls passed through the Home in a typical year. Reverend Herman D. Clarke—the aforementioned placing agent for the Children's Aid Society, made an entry in his journal regarding this Home:

"This is the Home where I sent girls for discipline when they could or would not keep their homes where placed. Here they were brought under strict control, and taught trades suitable for girls." Emily would later recall that she learned how to cane chairs and make brooms as a young girl, which likely took place at this Home.

Eventually it was determined that Emily should be sent for a trial placement in the home of a lady in New Rochelle, New York. However, after a short time, Emily was deemed "unsatisfactory," and was returned to the Elizabeth Home. She was then sent to Mrs. Hinley for "training." One can only imagine what that entailed, but it was customary for the Society to teach children table manners; how to brush their teeth daily; how to bathe properly, and how to lace shoes. Mrs. Hinley eventually approved of Emily "going to a western home."

Chapter Four

Emily Rides the Orphan Train

"Mr. Clarke, I want a little girl with curly black hair and black eyes, pleasant features, good form, a good singer, and a good memory, so as to take part in Sunday School concerts... and a complexion that will not tan or freckle in the sun."

- Application made by an Iowa woman for a child from the orphan train

A very big change was about to occur in Emily's life. On the morning of Tuesday, March 13th, 1906, Emily was picked up at the Elizabeth Home and taken to the United Charities Building, located in the northeast corner of Fourth Avenue and 22nd Street in Manhattan. This building was built in 1893 with funding provided by Joseph Stewart Kennedy, a wealthy New York businessman. The numerous charitable organizations that it housed included the Association for Improving the Condition of the Poor, the New York City Mission and Tract Society, The Charity Organization Society, and the Children's Aid Society offices, which were located on either side of the front entrance, and on a part of the 5th floor. Here, Emily and seven other children were gathered together from various orphanages and childcare agencies in Brooklyn and Manhattan. This was the usual practice of the

Children's Aid Society as they did not operate any orphanages themselves, per se. In fact, by the late 1890s, the Aid Society was almost exclusively obtaining children from public and private orphanages within New York City and the surrounding boroughs, as well as from upstate New York. In part, this practice came about because of the fact that the Aid Society suffered through several lawsuits that were initiated by parents of children who had been "recruited" from the streets of New York by agents of the Aid Society, and subsequently sent west on orphan trains without having acquired proper consent from the surviving parent or parents of the child. It was not uncommon for children to lie about being an orphan, especially if they wanted to escape some sort of abuse that was occurring at home. Since its inception, the Children's Aid Society really regarded the children, to put it in modern terms, as "independent contractors," and therefore did not put extreme emphasis on obtaining consent from parents of a child.

The United Charities Building at 4th Avenue and 22nd street, Manhattan, New York. (Harper's Weekly, September 26, 1891/Library of Congress)

In fact, the children themselves were often asked to sign forms of consent. The Aid Society simply felt that it was in the best interest of the child to be taken away from such parents, whatever the circumstances may have been.

Another reason that children were almost exclusively obtained from institutions was because the Aid Society had come under fire from various groups since its inception for ignoring the religious background of a child, and in particular, placing Catholic children in Protestant homes. Therefore, they took care to obtain children, whenever possible, from institutions that were predominantly Protestant. Such was the case with the Home for Destitute Children, from which Emily came.

In Emily's case, any rights of the parents were relinquished when she and her brother were seized by the Society for the Prevention of Cruelty to Children.

In addition to Emily, the little company of children consisted of Bernice Lindergren—the baby of the company at age one and a half; Kathleen Marie Belt, age nine; Amy Calhoun, age eight; Alfred Bauman, age three, who was brought from the Sheltering Arms Nursery on Dean Street in Brooklyn; Joseph Rowland, age three; Joseph's brother, Ira Rowland, age five; Samuel Orr, age unknown, and Gertrude Perry, age four. All of these children had one thing in common—they either had no families to go home to, or none that wanted them. Fate brought them all together on that cold March day in 1906. Little did they know that they would soon be taking part in the largest migration of children to ever occur in the history of the world.

The boys were soon instructed to get in an elevator, which would take them down to the basement where they would be taking a shower. When they finished, each one was fitted with a new set of clothes. The girls had already been fitted with wool dresses before their departure from the various children's institutions that had housed them. As was customary, each child was presented with a brand new copy of the Bible, as well as a hat, coat, and a pair of warm gloves.

An engraving depicting the placement of children in new homes in the West. (Harper's New Monthly Magazine)

Emily and the other children were then told they would be taking a train ride to their new homes and new families out West. They were made to believe that a real home, with a father and mother, was the nicest possible thing that they could have. The types of homes that awaited them were then described. Such news was generally met with enthusiasm by the youngest children or those who had lost both parents, but could be quite alarming to the older children who knew they had one or both parents living in the area. Such was the case with Emily. She just couldn't understand why she had to be sent off to a strange family when her parents or older siblings could simply come and get her if they had truly wanted to; though she had pretty much given up on any hope of them doing so many years earlier.

One former resident of the Elizabeth Home for Girls, from which Emily came, wrote to her friends back in New York after being sent West: "Now, my dear girls, I would advise you to come West, if you would like to be treated as one of the family. You are not treated as hired girls in the city—oh, no, if they go to town, you go—if they go off visiting, you go along."[1]

A former newsboy wrote to his old companions back in New York: "Do you want to be newsboys, always, and shoe-blacks, and timber-merchants in a small way by sellin' matches? If ye do you'll stay in New York, but if you don't you'll go West, and begin to be farmers, for the beginning of a farmer, my boys, is the making of a congressman, and a president."[2]

Though the rule was occasionally broken, it was the policy of the Children's Aid Society to not send any children on the trains after the age of fourteen. Charles Loring Brace, founder of the Aid Society, once commented on the challenges of placing girls between the ages of fourteen and eighteen…"a more difficult class than these to manage, no philanthropic mortal ever came in contact with."[3] He added that the older boys were inclined to "skip off" when too much pressure was applied. They were considered just too set in their ways and beyond any reform after a certain age. Emily just barely fell within the Aid Society's requirements, as she was just fifteen days shy of her fourteenth birthday.

The official destination of the company Emily was placed in was a town in Eastern Iowa named Hopkinton. Accompanying the group were two of the Children's Aid Society's agents—Reverend Herman D. Clarke, age 55, and Miss Anna Laura Hill, age 27.

Reverend Clarke had a slight figure, and was short in stature. Though he had brown hair as a young man, it was now receding and beginning to gray. He kept his hair short and neatly combed to the right. He lost his left eye in a freak accident when a young man, but he chose not to wear a patch over it, even though it was quite apparent that it was damaged. It appeared as if he was squinting, as the eye was always half closed. He was a soft-spoken man, but was always firm in his convictions. He believed, as Brace did, that one could achieve far better results by sitting down and reasoning with a child, rather than resorting to physical punishment.

Anna Laura Hill would be assisting Reverend Clarke. Anna was a resident of Elmira, New York. She began her employment with the Children's

Reverend Herman D. Clarke as a young man. He was a placing agent for the Children's Aid Society.
(Mrs. Walter Sayre)

Aid Society in 1902. Miss Hill wore glasses and was large in stature, which gave her a commanding presence. Her eyes of dark brown were large and round, but had a look of gentleness in them. Her brown hair was done up in a bun. She had a soft, round face. Her skin was very pale and baby smooth.

Though it was not customary to allow the children to take any personal belongings with them on the journey, Reverend Clarke would often allow them to do so. Some took their favorite books, a favorite doll or toy, or a photograph of a loved one. Possessions had been few in the orphanage.

Emily had but one thing that she cared to bring with her on her voyage—a little round brass pin with a photo of her dear father encased in it. She held it firmly in her hand, and as she sat waiting for their departure, she gazed down upon the face of her father, wondering if she would ever see him, her mother or any of her brothers and sisters again. She felt as if she was going to cry, but quickly regained her composure. She wanted to be brave for the younger children present.

Reverend Clarke bowed his head in prayer. Before departing with each group of children he would, as he would later write in his journals, "make each boy and girl, and each trip, the subject of a special prayer":

"Lord, these are thy little ones in need, and thou art the God of the orphan. Open the way for these."[4]

They then proceeded to load six or seven large boxes full of food for the trip, which included "loaves of graham and white bread, and all sorts of sandwich filling, such as ham, cheese, peanut butter, lettuce, celery, mayonnaise dressing, figs, dates, and raisins, apples, oranges and bananas, cakes and cookies, and cans of condensed milk for the younger children, and baby."[5]

The older children's clothing was carried in the Society's huge trunk, and the younger children each carried a small bundle of their belongings. Reverend Clarke and Miss Hill took their own personal trunks, as well as an emergency bag. The emergency bag contained "knives, forks, and spoons, bubs, towels, washcloths and soap, tooth paste, a sewing kit, and a Sterno burner to heat the milk for the baby. There were also blankets, and knitted shawls, medicine for colds, and coughs, burns, etc., as well as larkspur, in case a vermin [head lice] should escape the vigilant eye of the caretaker at the different homes."⁶

The children were marched out the office door and down the front steps of the United Charities Building to the horse-drawn streetcar that awaited them. The streetcar ride would be a new adventure for most of the children.

It was Tuesday noon and large snowflakes were falling ever so softly from the skies above, putting a pretty white blanket on everything below. The streetcar slowly made its way through the busy streets of Manhattan.

The driver carefully avoided getting anywhere near a new invention called the "automobile," as the noise they created caused many teams of horses to run away. They made their way to the Chamber Street boat slip

A horse-drawn streetcar such as the one that Emily and the other children would have rode on their way from United Charities building to the ferry, winds its way through the streets of Manhattan in 1908. (Corbis, BE076851)

A view of the Manhattan skyline from Jersey City—similar to the one Emily would have seen. This photo depicts the ferryboat "Washington" circa 1900-1910. (Library of Congress)

where a large ferryboat awaited them to take them to the Erie railroad and ferry terminal in Jersey City, New Jersey, which was located approximately one mile across the North River.

The ferry ride would be another new adventure for many of the children. As was customary, Reverend Clarke, Miss Hill and the children were allowed to board the boat ahead of all others so they could share adjoining seats. This assisted Reverend and Miss Hill in keeping a watchful eye on their little charges. As the boat chugged farther and farther out into the icy water, making its way towards the New Jersey shores, Emily undoubtedly took one last look at the Manhattan skyline, wondering if she would ever see it again.

Upon their arrival, they navigated the large and very busy railroad station and boarded a coach on the train that would take them on to Chicago, Illinois, where they would then transfer to a different rail line. The huge trunk was checked, and the emergency bag was taken out for the trip. The little company boarded the train, taking up nearly one whole side of one of the day coaches.

As late as 1910, no railroad coming from the south or the west had a direct connection to New York City—the largest city in the Western Hemisphere. The terminals of the railroads—whether the giant ones like the Pennsylvania and the Erie, or the minor ones, like the West Shore and the Susquehanna—stood on the New Jersey shore of the North River, the local name for this stretch of the Hudson. In Jersey City, Hoboken, and Weehawken, the major railroad companies built their large passenger stations at the edge of the river, which at that location was close to a mile wide. Numerous ferry routes connected these New Jersey stations to Manhattan; particularly to 23rd street, 14th street, Christopher Street, and Chambers Street in lower Manhattan.

The Pavonia Station where Emily and the others were taken was described as "brightly colored and styled in a Gothic image." The three-story terminal had a taller square tower at the corner that was topped by clocks on two sides and a widow's walk above. The waiting room facing the tracks was 66 by 1000 feet.

The railways often provided special cars, but most often the companies of orphans traveled in one of the day coaches. The railroads also provided discounted rates or even free passes for the transportation of the children. It was common for them to offer "one quarter fare for all under twelve years, and one half for older ones."[7] The agents and nurses would also receive special rates. Depending on the class of the ticket, the cost of the trip from Jersey City to Chicago would cost between seventy and one hundred twenty dollars per person in today's currency.

The Aid Society was often able to cover the costs of transporting the children through the generous donations of several prominent citizens of New York City.

Reverend Clarke and Miss Hill would now have a couple of long days and sleepless nights ahead of them. They would be kept constantly busy observing the children and assisting those who got motion sickness, or those who happened to fall out of their makeshift beds. For the larger groups of

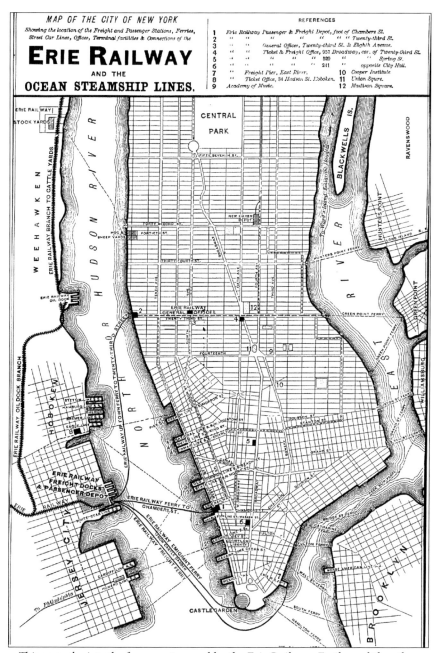

This map depicts the ferry routes used by the Erie Railway. Emily and the others departed from the Erie Passenger Depot located on lower left of map. (Erie Rail Way Company, 1874)

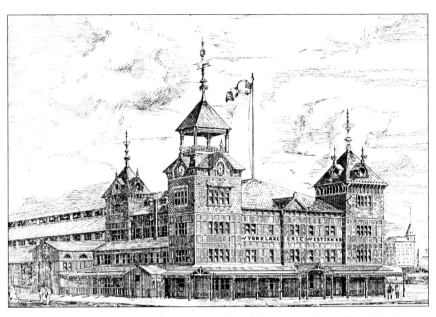

The New York, Lake Erie, and Western Railroad Station in Jersey City, New Jersey. Emily, like so many thousands of other orphan children, departed from this depot on an orphan train that would take them to their new homes in the West. (Walter G. Berg, C.E., 1893)

An example of one of the special railway passes used by Reverend Clarke when transporting the children. (Mrs. Walter Sayre) children there were often planks laid between the seats to facilitate them, but that would not be necessary for this size group. However, the hard horsehair seats were not much more comfortable.

"All aboard!" yelled the conductor, and with that, the train started to slowly chug its way in a northwesterly direction down the tracks, spewing steam high into the air above the engine.

The train made its way immediately to Newark and Morristown in New Jersey, and on to Stroudsburg and Scranton in northeastern Pennsylvania. It then crossed the border into Binghamton, New York. The next large city along the way would be Elmira, New York—the hometown of the assisting agent, Anna Laura Hill.

They then continued on through numerous small towns along southwestern New York, not far from the Pennsylvania border. They rolled through Hornell and Jamestown, and then turned southwesterly, towards the northwestern Pennsylvania cities of Corry and Meadville, several miles east-southeast of Erie. The train then crossed into east-central Ohio.

There was always the danger that the children would catch cold from exposure, as the train car was inadequately heated. It would be the job of Reverend Clarke and Miss Hill to fill the coal-burning stove that stood in the corner of the coach. A small bin adjacent to the stove held the coal. It barely provided enough heat for the large coach, and it inevitably left everyone and everything coated with a grimy layer of coal dust.

Reverend Clarke and Miss Hill would also need to stand careful guard over the cold water tank. They learned in the past that as the children became increasingly thirsty from the dry, dusty air inside the car, they would make frequent visits to the water tank, and would become ill from drinking the cold water too quickly.

The children often caught the attention of several of the other passengers in the coach. It was not unusual for people to give the children nickels and dimes on the trip, or offer to braid the hair of the girls. More often, they provided the children with candy and chocolate, which always kept the agents busy cleaning their faces and hands. Others gave donations to the Aid Society, which Reverend Clarke faithfully sent back to the main office.

The train continued west through the Ohio cities of Youngstown and Akron, Mansfield, Lima, and Ohio City, among many others. They rolled into the larger northeastern Indiana cities of Decatur and Huntington. The train stopped briefly at numerous stations along the tracks. Emily and several of the other children noted how the sleepy little towns they passed through stood in stark contrast to the skyscrapers they had grown up around in New York.

Though the wide assortment of food that the children were fed on the trip was well received by them, it caused many of them to suffer severe motion sickness. This was primarily due to the fact that so many of them had been suffering from malnutrition.

The trip often proved to be bittersweet for many of the children. Some were be excited about finally being able to be part of a family, yet others were fearful of the unknown. Some had to leave behind a dear friend, or a brother or sister with whom they were very close. To them, the trip often felt more like a forced exile than a new opportunity—a feeling that only intensified over time, as they slowly realized that there was little likelihood that they would ever be reunited with family and friends. Still, even while shedding tears, the children were full of questions about things they had never seen before as they traveled for the first time through rural America.

All the sights of the open country fascinated Emily and the other children. There were herds of cows and flocks of sheep grazing in farmers' fields, and horses galloping in the snow-covered meadows. The snow grew deeper the farther west they traveled. Farmers could be seen traveling on the country roads with their bobsleds. The children undoubtedly dreamed of getting off the train and making a snowman or throwing snowballs. Although they were allowed to get out and stretch at various stops along the way, they had to be careful not to soil their new set of clothes. And of course, time was of the essence. They had to keep moving on.

The train continued making its way northwesterly through the state of Indiana to the cities of Rochester and Hammond, located just south of Lake Michigan, a matter of miles south-southeast of the their final destination of Chicago.

Chicago was known as the "gateway to the West," and this was especially true for the many thousands of orphan children that would stop there to change trains before continuing on to their western destinations. The following article ran in a Chicago paper in 1899, and was syndicated across the country:

"SHIP 90,000 BABIES FROM NEW YORK CITY—

Chicago, Dec. 20—Some proof of the New York assertion that it can take care of its stray dogs better than of its waif babies is found in the statement of H. H. Hart of the Illinois Children's Home and Aid society, who says Father Knickerbocker has shipped 90,000 babies to the west since he began to think of some method of disposing of surplus children…The men and women who manage the Chicago exchange to which waif babies come and from which they are placed in homes say Chicago has five demands for every one it can fill with a baby. The men and women who deal with babies, as with commodities, have them ranked and classified. 'It's a strange thing,' said Mr. Hart, 'that when people want a baby of their own they want a boy. When they want to adopt one they want a girl. We could dispose of any number of pretty little girls. At the nursery in Englewood the other day we had twenty-four boys and only one girl. Boys from 4 to 8 years are hard to place. The demand is for them when they get a little older, and such demands are always subject to considerable investigation and some suspicion. The boys are apt to be wanted for the money they can earn for a family so we have to be careful."[8]

The train carrying Emily and the others rolled into Union Station shortly after noon on Friday, stopping at the entrance located in the northeast corner of South Canal and West Adams streets. They were greeted by a light snowfall driven by brisk northerly winds. The temperature hovered in the upper teens, which was cold, even for mid-March.⁹

Reverend Clarke led the company through the station. Miss Hill carried the baby, Bernice, and took up a position at the rear of the little line they had formed. Every precaution was made to not lose a child in the chaos of the crowded stations. Emily was well accustomed to walking single file from her days at the Home.

Reverend Clarke was always mindful of the time that he lost three girls at the station in 1904 when they were swept away by the crowds. Two of

Union Station, Chicago, Illinois. Note the horse-drawn Omnibuses that await passengers in front of the building. (Chicago Historical Society)

Waiting room at Union Station, Chicago, Illinois, as it appeared in 1906. (Chicago Historical Society)

the girls were subsequently found by the Reverend's wife on Dearborn Street. The third, a girl named Cornelia Smith, apparently walked some three miles away. She thought she was following Reverend Clarke the entire way, and ended up in a drug store. The police were notified and she was brought back "in a patrol wagon with two burley policeman."[10]

After the company's arrival in Hopkinton the itinerary called for the following:

The children would be taken to the Hotel Hopkinton where Reverend Clarke and Miss Hill would comb their hair and place ribbons in the hair of the girls. At about 10:30 a.m. the children would be marched to the dining hall of the Hopkinton Masonic Lodge, where the distribution was to take place. The children would be seated in a semi-circle.

Reverend Clarke would speak for about an hour at this point, explaining the goals and expectations of the Society. The children would be asked to step forward, one at a time, and the agent would give their name, nationality, traits, and other background information. On occasion, the children would be asked to sing a song, or otherwise perform for the audience. Twin sisters, Nettie and Nellie Crook, who rode an orphan train to Kansas in 1911, later recalled being asked to sing "Jesus Loves Me" for a group of prospective foster parents.[11]

The selection process often took a toll on the children. Being passed over repeatedly in favor of another child only served to reinforce existing feelings of loneliness and abandonment. Jack Voigt, who rode an orphan train to Kansas in 1920, likened the experience to "picking out puppies."[12]

Such an event would often draw prospective foster parents from as far away as thirty miles, and crowds of upwards of 1,500 people. One observer in an unidentified western town in 1912 noted: "The prairie town was as excited as if a convention were in session…Business men came to their doors; men and women hurried to join the parade [of children]…Three hundred interested persons had their attention fixed on the stage, and no show troupe ever had such intense attention as did the fourteen somewhat frightened kiddies who sat in a row behind the footlights. In the eyes of many women was a glisten of tears."[13]

The following poignant description of a distribution was made by Hastings H. Hart, in 1882:

> "I was myself a witness of the distribution of forty children in Nobles County, Minnesota, by my honored friend, Agent James Mathews…The children arrived at about half-past three p.m., and were taken directly from the train to the courthouse, where a large crowd was gathered. Mr. Mathews set the children, one by one, before the company, and, in his stentorian voice, gave a brief account of each. Applicants for children were then admitted in order behind the railing and rapidly made their selections. Then, if the child gave assent, the bargain was concluded on the spot. It was a pathetic sight, not soon to be forgotten, to see those children and young people, weary, travel-stained, confused by the excitement and unwonted surroundings, peering into those strange faces, and trying to choose wisely for themselves. And it was surprising how many happy selections were

made under such circumstances. In a little more than three hours, nearly all of those forty children were disposed of. Some who had not previously applied selected children. There was little time for consultation, and refusal would be embarrassing; and I know that the committee consented to some assignments against their better judgment."[14]

Reverend Clarke later recorded his thoughts on placing out children in one of his journals:

> "When a child goes to an industrial school, improvement is seen, and when taken to some good farm home they are new creatures. Their circumstances and environment is so changed that they too are changed for the better. Their morale is better, and this is a wonderful change.
>
> Regular work is given them, and they have the care of cows and horses. Girls have chickens to call their own, and there is a natural love of animals, and then there is a discipline and some religious influences, though not usually of the highest type, but enough to have much influence so that hidden tendencies are awakened to goodness. In a short time they are new boys and girls, as compared with the life they were living in the city."[15]

It was the policy of the Children's Aid Society to not place brothers and sisters in the same home, unless absolutely necessary. They feared sibling rivalry would cost them their new homes, and it often did. Of course, this caused many tearful separations.

After the first meeting adjourned, a second meeting would occur at about 2:00 p.m. in the afternoon. At this time, a local committee, which had been chosen prior to the arrival of the train, would assist in placing the children with interested parties. Often, very unusual requests for children were made to the agents. Reverend Clarke later recorded one example in his journals:

> "There were freaks among those who made application for children. Beauty seemed to be the first consideration or qualification, especially among men. Very many people seemed desirous to have a pretty girl to 'show off.' Not having enough children to satisfy all the applicants at New Sharon, Iowa in 1904, I received something like this:
>
> 'Mr. Clarke, I want a little girl with curly black hair and black eyes, pleasant features, good form, a good singer, and a good memory, so as to take part in Sunday school concerts, and a complexion that will not tan or freckle in the sun.' I never found the child!"[16]

After the placements were made, any remaining children would be taken on to the next town, or included in the next scheduled distribution. In some instances, usually because of sickness, unruliness, or a number of failed attempts at placement, children would be returned to New York. The agents would spend several days after each distribution paying visits to those families that took children. If all was deemed satisfactory, the children were allowed to remain in the homes.

Agents would often be summoned back at a later date if a placement was not working out. Reverend Clarke recorded one instance in his journals where he was called to remove a boy named Henry Schaupy who was taken with a company of children to Chatfield, Minnesota in 1903. His foster parents determined that he was displaying too much aggression after they observed him swatting a fly![17]

Reverend Clarke recorded:

> "People, I am obliged to say, expect more of an orphan child than they do of their own. Their faults seem greater. Are magnified greater. Some people are selfish in taking children. They just want a pet to dress up, show off, and doll up. They do not want any responsibility when they take a child, but expect all will be well and harmonious, and when a fault is seen they are too ready to have the child replaced, or sent

Homes Wanted
For Children.

A Company of Orphan Children of different ages in charge of

H. D. Clarke, Agt.

will arrive at your town

Thursday, May 4th.

The object of the coming of these children is to find homes in your midst, especially among farmers, where they may enjoy a happy and wholesome family life, where kind care, good example and moral training will fit them for a life of self-support and usefulness. They come under the auspices of the New York Children's Aid Society, by whom they have been tested and found to be well-meaning and willing boys and girls.

The conditions are that these children shall be properly clothed, treated as members of the family, given proper school advantages and remain in the family until they are eighteen years of age. At the expiration of the time specified it is hoped that arrangements can be made whereby they may be able to remain in the family indefinitely. The Society retains the right to remove a child at any time for just cause, and agrees to remove any found unsatisfactory after being notified.

Remember the time and place. All are invited. Come out and hear the address. Applications may be made to any one of the following well known citizens, who have agreed to act as local committee to aid the agent in securing homes.

A typical dodger used to advertise the coming of the orphan children in the weeks just prior to the event. (Mrs. Walter Sayre) back to the Aid Society. The stealing of a cookie, or the telling of a lie, has caused some to lose their homes. I was sent for to take away a boy of ten years for the awful crime of going in the cellar and sticking his fingers in some jelly. Would they send away their own child for that?"[18]

In some cases, the children would run away before Reverend Clarke could make it to the home to investigate the complaints made against the child. A few children were lucky enough to fit in so well in their new home that they were eventually adopted. Such was the case with a little girl named Gertrude L. Bell who was placed by Reverend Clarke in Welton, Iowa on May 23, 1905. Gertrude's photo, the paperwork given to the foster parents upon her placement, and Gertrude's adoption papers are reproduced on the next few pages.

Reverend Clarke had received a letter from Mr. and Mrs. Carlton U. Parker—some friends of his in Chicago who were interested in taking a girl into their home. He had subsequently requested that the Parkers meet him at Union Station to look the group of children over. The Parkers stood in the large waiting room at the station and conversed with the children for some time. Emily found them both very charming and felt that they would provide a very good home for her. After all, she was used to city life and was certain that she would be much happier living in the city, rather than in a farmer's home in the country. She stepped forward and

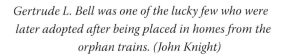

Gertrude L. Bell was one of the lucky few who were later adopted after being placed in homes from the orphan trains. (John Knight)

The placing agent would hand each set of foster parents an envelope that held a card (bottom) that outlined the Terms and Conditions that the child was placed under, as well as a card (top) that gave personal information about the child (Gertrude L. Bell) who was born May 20, 1903 (wrongly given as 1905), and placed on May 23, 1905 in Welton, Iowa. (John Knight)

EMIGRATION DEPARTMENT OF THE
Children's Aid Society of New York.
CENTRAL OFFICE UNITED CHARITIES BUILDING
105 East 22d Street, New York City.

The Society reserves the right to remove a child at any time for just cause.

Date of placing *May 23, 1905*
Name of child *Gertrude L. Bell*
Age *2 yrs. May 20 1905*
H. D. Clark AGENT.

Terms on Which Children are Placed in Homes

Applicants must be endorsed by the Local Committee. The child selected may then be taken to the home for mutual acquaintance, but no permanent arrangement will be considered until the home has been visited by the Placing-out Agent of the Society and the necessary papers signed.

Children under 14 years of age if not legally adopted, must be retained as members of the family, schooled according to the Educational Laws of the State, and comfortably clothed until they are 18 years old. It is then expected that suitable provision will be made for their future.

Children between 14 and 16 years of age must be boarded and clothed until they are 18 when they are at liberty to make their own arrangements.

Children over 16 years of age may be taken on a mutual agreement witnessed by the Agent of the Society or by a member of the local committee.

Parties taking children agree to make reports of them to the Society twice a year, and to urge the children, if old enough, to write also. Removals of children proving unsatisfactory can be arranged through the local committee or an Agent of the Society, the party agreeing to retain the child a reasonable length of time after notifying the Society of the desired change.

declared her desire to go home with the Parkers, eager for the chance to finally have a mother and father.

Reverend Clarke discussed Emily's request briefly with Miss Hill and the Parkers, and he then gave his consent. Emily said her goodbyes to the Reverend, Miss Hill, and the other children. She and the Parkers then disappeared into the vast crowd at the station.

A Station Agent paid special attention to the curious group, and escorted Reverend Clarke, Miss Hill, and the remaining children to a horse-drawn Frank Parmelee omnibus that would take them to the Chicago, Milwaukee and St. Paul train station. This station held the train that would take them on to Hopkinton, Iowa. Hopkinton was located in Delaware County, about 35 miles west-southwest of Dubuque, not far over the Illinois border.

O. WILLIS JAMES, PRESIDENT.
CHARLES E. WHITEHEAD, VICE-PRESIDENT.
A. B. HEPBURN, TREASURER.
C. LORING BRACE, SECRETARY.

Children's Aid Society,
UNITED CHARITIES BUILDING,
105 EAST 22ND STREET,
TELEPHONE, 899 18TH STREET.

New York, September 12th, 190 7.

THIS IS TO CERTIFY, that Gertrude L. Bell, who was born May 30th, 1903, being a dependent child, was surrendered to the CHILDREN'S AID SOCIETY OF NEW YORK, (a corporation duly incorporated under the Laws of the State of New York, and having its principal offices in the City of New York,) to be provided with a permanent home till of age; that the said child was accordingly placed by an Agent of the said Society with Frank T. Arrington, and Sarah E. Arrington, his wife, of Welton, Clinton County, Iowa, and the said CHILDREN'S AID SOCIETY does hereby consent to the legal adoption of the said child by the said Frank T. Arrington and his wife, subject to the approval of the Surrogate or County Judge of the County of Clinton, in the State of Iowa, as provided by law.

AND the said Frank T. Arrington and Sarah E. Arrington his wife, of Welton, Clinton County, Iowa, aforesaid, do hereby undertake and agree, in pursuance of the provisions of the laws of the State of Iowa, to adopt and treat the said minor child as their own lawful child.

IN WITNESS WHEREOF, the said CHILDREN'S AID SOCIETY has caused this instrument to be attested by its Secretary, CHARLES L. BRACE, who is authorized by the Board of Directors of said Society to sign its corporate name to the above and similar instruments, and has caused its corporate seal to be hereunto affixed, this 12th day of September in the year of our Lord, One Thousand Nine Hundred and Seven; and likewise the said Frank T. Arrington and Sarah E. Arrington, his wife, have hereunto affixed their hands and seals this 19th day of September in the year of our Lord, One Thousand Nine Hundred and Seven.

Children's Aid Society
by *Charles L. Brace*
Secretary.

Frank T. Arrington
Sarah E. Arrington

Adoption papers for Gertrude L. Bell. (John Knight)

STATE OF NEW YORK, } ss.
COUNTY OF NEW YORK, }

On this 18th day of September in the year One Thousand Nine Hundred and Seven before me personally came CHARLES L. BRACE, to me personally known, who being by me duly sworn, did depose and say, that he resides in New York; that he is the Secretary of the CHILDREN'S AID SOCIETY, the corporation described in and which executed the foregoing certificate; that he knew the corporate seal of the CHILDREN'S AID SOCIETY; that the seal affixed to the foregoing instrument was such corporate seal; that it was so affixed by order of the Board of Trustees of the said corporation, and that he signed his name thereto by the like order, as Secretary of said corporation.

C. I. C. Opit
NOTARY PUBLIC
for the City and County of New York.

STATE OF IOWA, } ss.
COUNTY OF CLINTON. }

On this 19th day of September in the year One Thousand Nine Hundred and seven before me personally came Frank T. Arrington and Sarah E. Arrington, his wife, both to me known, and known to me to be the individuals described in and who executed the foregoing instrument, and they thereupon duly and severally acknowledged to me that they executed the same.

J. H. Evans Jr.
Notary Public.

Adoption papers for Gertrude L. Bell. (John Knight)

It was another day and night before the train arrived in Hopkinton. Reverend Clarke immediately sat down after the distribution took place and penned a letter to the Aid Society on Hotel Hopkinton stationery regarding Emily's placement, among other things:

> "All placed but one and that one bids fair to be placed. A friend in Chicago, C. U. Parker. 2644 Chicago Ave. (Sub) wrote me some time ago about taking a girl. He has no children. He is a fine Christian man, & wife of excellent family. He is city inspector of walks. He wants to go out of city to some fruit farm. Mr. and Mrs. Parker met us at Union Station, and we talked the matter over. Emily Reese wanted to go with them. I consented and she is there on trial and subject to our further investigation. If you know of any Illinois law against it, then I can quickly remove her. We placed 'Herbert Welch' there two years ago 'you know.'
>
> Mr. Parker is a well-educated man, and I have read fine articles from his pen. If there is any hitch about this procedure, let me know. Emily will have good advantages, and refined & Christian influences, if she stays in that home. I know as yet, nothing of Emily's disposition. Yours, H. D. C."

A Parmelee style omnibus, such as the one used by Reverend Clarke to transport companies of children between train stations, is seen here unloading a group of emigrants at the Chicago and Northwestern Station on Wells street in Chicago. (Northwestern Bulletin, June 1909/Northern Illinois University)

In his letter written at the Hotel Hopkinton, Reverend Clarke alluded to the possibility that there may be a problem with Emily's placement in the State of Illinois per the state laws at the time. An 1899 Illinois newspaper article addressed the subject: "…Illinois and other western states have made the baby export business of New York a subject for special legislation, putting a stop to it in many cases. The legislature of Illinois passed an act at the last session, putting a stop to it. Consequently, New York is now sending more babies to New England instead of the West, as heretofore."[19]

The placing agents generally tried to make visits to the new foster families with whom the children were placed within several days following their placement. A horse and buggy would be rented at the local livery stable for this purpose.

There were often very affecting scenes during these routine visits. Reverend Clarke wrote of one such instance that occurred just two months prior to his arrival in Hopkinton:

> "Princeton, Missouri Company of January 18th, 1906—In this company was Clara Schmidt from the Gallatin, Missouri party. She was placed a little later, and was a pathetic case. When reaching the home where I was to leave her, she would not stay, but ran out and climbed into the carriage, and I had to take her into the house again. Again she escaped, and grabbed hold of the carriage wheel as I attempted to drive off. Again I took her in, and when starting away, she ran down the road following the liveryman and myself, crying, 'Oh, Mr. Clarke, take me with you. I want to go with you.' I stopped the horses, and told the liveryman that I must go back and do it all over again. Getting out of the carriage, I approached her, when suddenly she stopped, and holding her hands up, said, 'Go on Mr. Clarke.' She ran back at once to her home, and was contented. A year or so later, when I had one lone girl to place in the community, that liveryman refused to go with me, saying he'd never go through that scene again."[20]

In re Emily Reese,

HOT WATER HEATED   **GOOD SAMPLE ROOMS**

HOTEL HOPKINTON
W. R. REEVE, Proprietor

$\frac{41}{388}$ #3993

Hopkinton, Iowa_____190____

All placed but one and that one bids fair to be placed

A friend in Chicago, C. V. Parker, 2644 Chicago Ave, (Sub) wrote me some time ago about taking a girl. He has no children. He's a very fine Christian man, & wife of excellent family. He is city inspector of walks. He wants to go out of city to some fruit farm. Mr. & Mrs. Parker met us at Union Station and we talked the matter over. Emily Reese wanted to go with them. I consented and she is there on trial and subject to our further investigation. If you know of any Illinois law against it, then I can quickly remove her. He placed "Hobert Welch" there two years ago "you know". Mr. Parker is a well educated man and I have read fine articles from his pen. If there is any hitch about this procedure let me know.

Emily will have good & advantageous and refined & Christian influences if she stays in that home. I know as yet nothing of Emily's disposition.

Yours,
H. D. C.

Say — read carefully enclosed article to Mr. Brace. What do you think of such satanic editing?

Letter written by Reverend H.D. Clarke to the Children's Aid Society regarding Emily's placement in Chicago. (Children's Aid Society)

The Hopkinton, Iowa Company of March 15, 1906. Agents H. D. Clarke and Anna Laura Hill are in back. Miss Hill is holding Bernice Lindergren. The girl in back center is Kathleen Marie Belt. Center row, left to right: Alfred Bauman, Amy Calhoun, Joseph Rowland, Ira Rowland, and Gertrude Perry. Child on front left is Samuel Orr. Emily Reese is absent as she was placed in Chicago on the way out. Photo taken in Hopkinton, Iowa. (Mrs. Walter Sayre)

Emily's situation was unique in the sense that hers was a single placement and not part of a group distribution. It was not until April 9th, 1906—nearly a month after she was placed, that Reverend Clarke was able to visit Emily's new home back in Chicago. Following his visit, he filed this report to the Children's Aid Society:

"Very pretty home. Mr. Parker built it, and owns it. Has lived there about 13 years. Solid man. Home well furnished. I think girl better suited than with average farm boys in the home on a farm. Thus far she has pleased them, and is quiet and modest, and says she will do her best to keep such a good home, and kind friends. Calls them 'aunt' and 'uncle.' Mrs. Parker seems to have tact. But of course, time must tell the story."

By the end of the summer, just as Emily was getting used to her new home, Mrs. Parker became ill. Doctors soon informed her that she had a tumor, as well as a heart condition.

It was a very hard decision for them to make, but they decided it was best if they gave Emily up. Emily was devastated, as she was just getting settled into her new home and was beginning to bond with the Parkers. Reverend Clarke was informed of their decision and quickly left on the train from his home in Dodge Center, Minnesota.

On August 22, 1906 Reverend Clarke placed Emily with the Cornelius Henry Pelham family of Malone, Iowa. Mr. Pelham was known as "Neal" to his friends and family. He had married the former Daisy Dean Duke on October 27, 1897, at De Witt, Iowa and they had a seven year-old son named Arthur.

Malone was located in Clinton County, about eighteen miles from the Illinois border in east-central Iowa. The Pelhams farmed 120 acres in Eden Township, about a mile and half outside of Malone. They were part of an extended family which consisted of several other farmers who resided nearby.

Emily spent about five months at the Pelham home when Reverend Clarke paid them a visit on January 24, 1907. He found Emily's relationship with the Pelham's "fairly agreeable." Emily was attending school and helping with the housework. Reverend Clarke reported:

> "A hired girl made some trouble with Emily by quizzing all about her past life, which Mrs. Pelham thinks was untruthful. Emily did not seem quite as well satisfied as at first, but said she liked the place. Had had some trouble with the little boy in the home. She does finely in school says teacher, and Mrs. Pelham."

Children's Aid Society,

(PLACING-OUT DEPARTMENT.)

United Charities Building,   105 EAST 22nd STREET, NEW YORK.

I, the undersigned, __C.H.Pelham,__ __Malone, Iowa,__ hereby agree to provide for __Emily Reese__, aged __13__ years, according to the following terms and conditions, and with the full understanding that the Society reserves the right to remove the child previous to legal adoption if at any time the circumstances of the home become such as in the judgment of the agent are injurious to the physical, mental or moral well-being of the child.

The terms and conditions for the retention of the girl in my family being as follows:—To care for her in sickness and in health, to send her to school during the entire free school year until she reaches the age of 14 years, and thereafter during the winter months at least, until she reaches the age of 16 years; also to have her attend Church and Sunday School when convenient, and to retain her as a member of my family until she reaches the age of 18 years. In case she proves unsatisfactory, I agree to notify the Society, and pending her removal, to keep her a reasonable length of time after such notice has been given. I agree, moreover, to use my best endeavor then and at all times to detain her should she try to leave me, until the Society can take steps for her removal. I agree to keep her at all times as well supplied with clothing as she was when I received her. I agree to write to the Society at least once a year.

Mr. C.H. Pelham

Witness, __H.D.Clarke,__

Agent,

Date, __August, 22nd.__ 190 6.

It is also agreed that the girl shall not be taken to any distant state before adoption without consent of the Society, nor to any hotel or restaurant for a home or work.

The original release form, as signed by Mr. Pelham. (Children's Aid Society)

This new foster home was not to be either. On March 21st, 1907, just two months after his visit, Reverend Clarke was summoned by the Pelham's to come and replace Emily because she "quarreled so with Mr. Pelham's little boy, and was saucy."

Life in the Home back in Brooklyn was so regimented that it left Emily ill-prepared to deal with real world circumstances. And of course, life on the farm was vastly different from life in the big city. Making the adjustment was not easy, and as time went on, things would only get worse for her.

Emily was soon to accompany Reverend Clarke to the home of Mr. and Mrs. Brown of Le Claire, Iowa. Le Claire was a river town located along the bluffs on the western bank of the Mississippi River in Scott County. It was about eighteen miles southeast of Emily's former home with the Pelham's in Malone. Le Claire happened to be the birthplace of the famous William "Buffalo Bill" Cody.

Mr. Brown was a carpenter as well as a farmer. They had two sons: Ralph, age twenty, and Clyde, age eighteen. Reverend Clarke reported:

The little depot at Le Claire, Iowa is nestled under the branches of an ancient Elm tree, and sits on the banks of the mighty Mississippi River. Emily and Reverend Clarke arrived here in the early months of 1907.

"Mr. Brown's home is pleasant, and girl seemed pleased. Piano in home, and the grown boys <u>appear</u> gentlemanly. I hope girl will do better."

The fact that the Reverend underlined the word "appear" seemed to indicate that he had some apprehension. And as it turned out, it was well founded.

On January 8, 1908, about ten months after being placed with the Browns, Reverend Clarke was again summoned to remove Emily. She was then just two months shy of her sixteenth birthday. Reverend Clarke reported:

"In the home with Brown's, Le Claire, she was robbed of the years' school, and her clothes. She promises to do her best now."

Years later, Reverend Clarke recalled this placement in his journals:

> "In the third home she was not well clothed, and again I took her. In doing so, her foster brother, in a great wrath, made terrible threats that he thought was enough to put me in silence regarding her being neglected by them. Years later this young man had charge of a lighthouse in Florida, and he wrote asking forgiveness for his rudeness, but wanted to know where his 'only sister he ever had' was. This I declined to give, but I frankly forgave him."

The train tracks would next carry Emily to the home of the Edwin P. Kellogg family in Lansing Township, Allamakee County, Iowa. Lansing was another river town, located in the extreme northeastern corner of Iowa. The state of Wisconsin could be seen across the river, and the state of Minnesota was just twelve miles to the north. The landscape in this part of Iowa consisted of steep-sided hills, many of which were covered with oaks, hickory, maple and basswood trees. Cold, fast running streams dashed through deep, narrow, limestone coulees—the deeply eroded remnants of a vast plateau composed of the fossilized floors of seas that came and went some 350 to 550 million years earlier.

Many of the town's homes and businesses were constructed using the local limestone. Others were built in the style of Victorian and Greek revival architecture.

The Kelloggs farmed 226 acres and were in their mid-thirties. They had three children: Harold, age eleven; Bernice, age six; and Cecil, age two. Reverend Clarke wrote of the Kelloggs:

"This is a most excellent Christian family from all appearances, and recommendations."

The Children's Aid Society requested that the children write to them at least twice a year, report on how they were doing, and perhaps send a photograph. The Society would often ask specific questions of the children. Emily wrote just such a letter during her stay with the Kelloggs on the day after Christmas 1908. The quaint letter is still on file at the Children's Aid Society. Emily wrote positively, if not grammatically, about her life:

> "Dear Sir,
>
> I received your letter quite a while ago, but did not answer. I go to school with the children that I live with. I stay at home & help with the work. I have not any photograph to sent. We live 2 ½ miles South East of Waukon. I do not know of the future years what I am going to do. I think I will be a dressmaker. I believed I will start to sew next summer. Well, I will close this time.
>
> Your Truly,
> Emily Reese
> Waukon, Iowa"

A year and five months passed before Reverend Clarke next visited Emily. He arrived on May 20th, 1909 and subsequently filed this report:

> "The family talks of moving into Wisconsin, and will take girl if consent is given. I gave hearty consent. Not far from State line. Wisconsin law cannot keep a family who has taken a girl from moving into the state <u>with her</u>. Anyway, she's self-supporting.

> Waukon Iowa
> Dec, 26, 1908.
>
> Dear Sir:
> I received your letter quite awhile ago but did not answer. I go to school with the children that I live with. I stay at home & help with the work. I have not any photograph to sent.
>
> We live 2½ miles south east of Waukon. I do not know of the future years what I am going to do — I think I will be a dressmaker. I beleived I will start to sew next summer. Well I will close this time
>
> Your Truly
> Emily Reese.
> address.
> Waukon Iowa
> c/o E. P. Kellogg.

A two-page letter written by Emily Reese to the Children's Aid Society on the day after Christmas, 1908. (Children's Aid Society)

"Emily is now a good Christian girl in present appearance, and profession. It was lucky I removed her from two past homes, and placed her here. Unless we are deceived, she will make a fine woman. She wants to take a nurses course in a Sanitarium, and Kelloggs will help her."

One night in the fall of 1909, nearly two years after Emily was placed with them, the Kelloggs attended a Seventh Day Adventist camp meeting in the woods near Waukon. All seemed to be going well, but the Kelloggs had other plans. At some point they decided they would be leaving without Emily. They waited until dark, and as soon as Emily was out of sight, they quietly slipped away.

Emily searched frantically for them, but to no avail. Finally, one of the men at the meeting told Emily that he recalled seeing them ride off into the night. Emily did not show her emotions immediately, but walked just out of the glow of the campfires and slumped down behind a large oak tree. She buried her face in her hands and sobbed.

As she slowly regained her composure she found strength in recalling the words that were painted on a small wooden sign that had hung in her classroom at the Home for Destitute Children:

A camp meeting typical of the one where Emily was deserted.
(Milton (WI) Historical Society)

"Success"
Just Look Ahead
Give Your Best
Keep on Trying
That's The Test

Life had dealt Emily yet another cruel blow. Would she ever find the happiness that she so longed for? Only time would tell.

Emily was taken home by one of the families who had attended the meeting that evening. First thing the next morning, they sent word to Reverend Clarke regarding Emily's predicament.

A very familiar scene then repeated itself. Reverend Clarke's hometown of Dodge Center, Minnesota was not that far away, and he soon left for Waukon to replace Emily once again.

The Reverend comforted Emily the best he could, but her spirit was clearly broken. Her next

CHILDREN'S AID SOCIETY,
PLACING-OUT DEPARTMENT,
UNITED CHARITIES BUILDING,
105 EAST 22ND STREET, NEW YORK.

Report of Visit to a Ward of the Society.

No.	Vol.	Page.	When Placed.
3993	41	388	1906

Name of Child: Emily Reese
Age: 16
Date Visited: 6/20/09

With Whom Placed: E.P. and Mary Kellogg,
Post Office Address: Waukon,
County: Allamakee
State: Iowa
Nearest Station: Waukon
Railroad: C M & St P
Distance and Direction from Station to the Home: 3 miles S E
Distance from Home to the School: about a mile
What is acreage of place, and is it owned or rented by foster parents: Rents farm
What is occupation of the head of the family: Farming

How many children in family—
Boys. Ages. | Girls. Ages.
Three children small - two boys and a girl

Number of persons, including hired help, now living at home: Six

Condition of the home as to—
Cleanliness: Good
Order: Good
Comfort: Good

Appearance of house, yard, barn, etc.: Average good

Is the home adapted to the child: Yes indeed

A report filed by H. D. Clarke to the Children's Aid Society regarding the placement of Emily Reese with the E. P. Kellogg family of Waukon, Iowa. (Children's Aid Society)

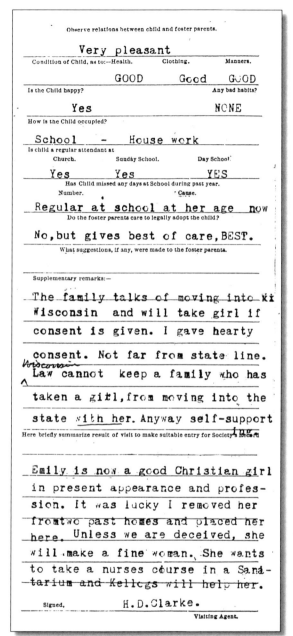

home would be her sixth or seventh foster home in five years, in no less than four states!

They soon reached the depot and boarded the train. It was Wednesday, September 1, 1909. The train gradually made its way east towards the mighty Mississippi River and snaked its way along the base of the majestic bluffs that soared high above the river's western edge.

The bluffs were formed some 12,000 years earlier by the runoff from the last of the glaciers—the Wisconsin. Several glaciers were steered clear of the area by the resistant ancient rock, as well as the deep basins of Green Bay, Lake Superior, and Lake Michigan. The melting ice widened the river valleys and carved deeply into the limestone bedrock, forming the great Mississippi River. The Paleo-Indians once hunted wooly mammoth and giant bison on the tops of these very bluffs at the end of the Ice Age.

Emily remembered how she had marveled at the beauty of the river and the bluffs when she crossed it on her westward journey into Iowa, and during her stay at Le Claire some three years earlier. This time she was heading east, back over the river. The bluffs slowly disappeared behind them as the train made its way deeper into the rolling hills and forests of Wisconsin. The leaves on the trees were ablaze with bright hues of red, yellow, and orange.

Wisconsin officials had been very vocal opponents of the placing out system over the years. At the 1874 meeting of the National Prison Reform Congress a delegate from Wisconsin, probably Hiram H. Giles, proclaimed "It is a misdemeanor to scatter and sow noxious weeds on the prairies and in the openings of Wisconsin, but it is 'Moral Strategy' to annually scatter *three thousand* obnoxious, 'iron-clad orphans,' juvenile criminals among the peaceful homes and in the quiet neighborhoods of the state."[21] At a meeting of the National Conference of Charities and Correction in 1882, Mr. E. Andrew Elmore, who had always been a supporter of the Children's Aid Society policies proclaimed: "I do not doubt but the intentions of the Society are good… But when they have placed these children in the West, do they look after them a moment? Not any. They get them off their hands and that ends the story…[I]t would be as well if you cut their jugular veins in the first place."[22]

Reverend Clarke had arranged to place Emily in the home of Mr. and Mrs. Charles H. Mikkelson of Milton Junction, Rock County, Wisconsin. He had friends living in the Milton area, which was founded in the 1840s by fellow Seventh Day Baptists from his native New York state.

Milton Junction was located about twenty-five miles north of the Illinois border in south-central Wisconsin. The Mikkelsons rented eighty-five acres of land within the mile between the towns of Milton and Milton Junction. Milton was home to the very well known Milton College, which was also founded by Seventh Day Baptists.

The Mikkelsons had two sons: Harold, age thirteen, and Paul, age five. Emily was now nearly seventeen and a half years old. Reverend Clarke filed this report with the Aid Society:

> "Ready for High School. The family at Waukon, Iowa were to move, and had no use for Emily. This new home wanted her, and will educate her right along in school. I placed her in Wisconsin as a <u>self-supporting</u> girl, and for her better education. She thanks me much, and is happy over it. Will need no more visits."

No more visits! Emily was on her own now. This would be her final foster home, and though she didn't know it yet, she was to live out the rest of her life in the Milton area. Nor did she have any way of knowing that her troubles were far from over.

Reverend Clarke made the following entry in his journal regarding this period in Emily's life:

> "I brought her into Wisconsin to another family of the same faith [the Mikkelson's were Seventh Day Adventists, as were the Kelloggs], and later she was coaxed away from her home by a family of the same church, and they urged her to go to South Dakota, where their people had a Sanitarium."

The family who coaxed Emily away was the Courtney family. In April 1910, after eight months with the Mikkelsons, Emily went to work as a hired girl at the farm home of George and Della Courtney, which stood in Janesville Township, just a few miles west-southwest of Milton Junction. The farm was located in the southeast corner of the intersection of County Trunk H and Cross (now Milton Townline) Road, near a little pond called Cross' Pond.

Emily was now eighteen years old. At the Courtneys she helped with various chores on the farm, which included hand-milking eight cows.

Despite the fact that the Courtneys had sons old enough to help with the chores, it often fell on Emily to keep the cows milked. Emily had learned how to milk cows well at some of the former farms she was placed on. It was just one of the many duties she had to learn to do on the farm, all of which were so very different from the lifestyle she knew back in New York.

She would later recall that if the Courtney boys didn't feel like it, they would even make her walk out into the pasture to herd the cows back to the barn so that she could then milk them! She also recalled how the Courtneys would take their children out for an ice cream cone, but they would refuse to buy one for Emily. She would have to sit and watch while the others enjoyed their treat.

In spite of her various trials in the Courtney home, Emily forged a life-long friendship with the family, and would later give two of her children middle names after members of the Courtney family. Emily would later recall how Mrs. Courtney taught her how to cook well. The pair entered many baking contests, and came away winners from a good many of them.

Emily attended the nearby Otterbein United Brethren Church (known to the locals as the Sandy Sink Church) with the Courtneys. Services were preached by the Reverend Charles J. Roberts, a circuit-riding minister. The church stood a short distance north of the Courtney farm on the crest of one of the many rolling hills in the area.

Emily joined the church choir and enjoyed it very much. She was a beautiful singer according to one Earl Kidder, whom we'll soon learn more about.

Chapter Five
A Romance Blossoms

"She threw her arms around my neck and jumped off the ground repeatedly, yellin', "Oh, Will ya?, Will ya?, Will ya?."

- Earl Kidder

Residing about two miles north of the Courtney family was the Clark and Elma Kidder family, which consisted of four sons and one daughter. Their names, in order of birth, were Rex, Leta, Bill, Earl, and Clark Junior (called Tot). The third oldest son, Earl Dane Kidder, was nearly seventeen, having been born at their Fulton farm home on March 25th, 1893.

After returning home from Janesville where he went to sell a load of cordwood to the jail, Earl's father, Clark, spied Emily walking alongside the road and offered her a ride home in his buggy. Upon his arrival home, Clark remarked to his son Earl, "I just met the sweetest young girl with the darkest eyes I've ever seen, and she's real smart. She's just a little bit of a thing. If I were a young man, I'd look her up."

It so happened that Earl's mother, Elma, was to host the next Ladies Aid Society meeting, and among those attending would be Mrs. Courtney and her new hired girl, Emily Reese. It was at this party that Earl would meet the girl his father spoke so highly of.

It just so happened that Earl recently purchased a fancy new rubber-tired buggy "for haulin' the girls around," at the North Western Carriage Company in Fort Atkinson, Wisconsin. Though he was painfully shy, Earl eventually worked up the nerve to ask Mrs. Courtney if it was okay to give Emily a ride "around the block" in his new buggy. Mind you, this was a country block, and amounted to about four miles!

To Earl's delight, Mrs. Courtney agreed, as long as they returned by four o'clock that afternoon. The young couple spent the time getting acquainted. That evening there happened to be a Medicine Show at the P. of H. (Patrons of Husbandry) Hall in Milton Junction, and Emily asked if she could accompany Earl to it. Mrs. Courtney agreed, setting a ten o'clock curfew.

Earl's father, Clark Dodge Kidder. (Courtesy of the author)

The Medicine Show had deep roots in America's history. They reached their heyday in the decades between 1870 and 1920. The lack of well-educated doctors, and the public's distrust of those who were, allowed the Medicine Shows to flourish. A typical show featured music, comedy, juggling, and overblown rhetoric, mixed with testimonials and stunts to demonstrate cures. Admission was free, with the performers making a living from the sale of cure-alls. The show promoters would often target sleepy farming communities, as they were always eager for any kind of entertainment.

The Clark and Elma Kidder home where Earl and Emily first met. Earl's mother, Elma, is seen here with Earl's brother, Bill. (Courtesy of the author)

The shows generally lasted about two hours, with the first two-thirds of the show being reserved for entertaining. When the entertainment ended, the pitch-doctor began his routine. He was often clad in a top hat, brocaded vest, and a frock coat. Dr. Thomas Kelley—a famous Canadian medicine show star who toured the United States, would remind his listeners:

> "You are all dying, every man, woman, and child is dying; from the instant you are born you begin to die and the calendar is our executioner. That, no man can hope to change…
>
> "Ponder well my words, then ask yourselves the question: Is there a logical course to pursue? Is there some way you can delay, and perhaps for years, that final moment before your name is written down by a bony hand in the cold diary of death? Of course, there is, ladies and gentlemen, and that is why I am here."[1]

The P of H (Patrons of Husbandry) Hall in Milton Junction, Wisconsin where Earl and Emily attended the Medicine Show. It is the large building in the center with a chimney at each end. (Milton (WI) Historical Society)

Most of these medicines were at best harmless; though others contained generous quantities of alcohol, opium, or cocaine, ensuring a quick feeling of well-being for the first-time customers, which was unfortunately followed by the possibility of habitual use.

Earl and Emily knew the routine, and like so many others in the community, simply attended the Show for the entertainment aspect of the event.

Emily's first date with a boy had gone pretty well. She returned to the Courtney home that evening just aglow with happiness.

A romance soon blossomed between the city girl and the farm boy, despite the fact that Earl had been going steady for many years with his childhood sweetheart, Minnie Beutow. In fact, Earl was unofficially engaged to be married to her. Earl would later recall Minnie was a "tall good-sized blonde." It seems Minnie's father had disliked Earl though, and it put quite a strain on the relationship. He often referred to Earl as "the damn Yankee." Beutow was a southerner. Minnie often sang with Emily, along with their mutual friend, Florence Nelson, in the choir at the Sandy Sink

Church. Earl would later fondly recall listening to them all sing Christmas carols on Christmas Eve.

Earl and Emily's brief romance came to a halt when Emily decided to leave the Courtneys at their urging, and head for Chamberlain, South Dakota, where she was given the opportunity to study to become a nurse at a sanitarium operated by Seventh Day Adventists. The Kelloggs had told her about the place and intended to send her there, prior to her abandonment

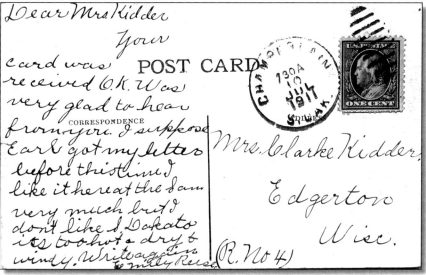

This is a postcard that Emily sent to Earl's mother during her stay in Chamberlain, South Dakota. (Courtesy of the author)

by them at the camp meeting. Emily remembered hearing about the sanitarium from the Kelloggs and wanted to give it a try after the Courtneys spoke of it. She and Earl kept in touch though, and exchanged several letters while Emily was away. The postcard on the previous page makes reference to one such letter.

Emily later recalled how her peers questioned her age upon her arrival at the sanitarium, thinking she was surely not a day over twelve, instead of the eighteen years she proclaimed she was. She was very small in stature you see—standing just four feet ten inches tall. Her eyes were very dark brown and her hair was jet black.

She was put in charge of four children at the sanitarium, and walked nearly a mile to work each day. She was not supplied any schoolbooks on the subject of nursing, which were required as part of her training. She knew the Courtneys did not have the money to send her, and she didn't feel as if it were proper to ask the Kidder family, as she had not known them that long. The only other person she could turn to was her guardian minister, Reverend Clarke:

This postcard depicts the Seventh Day Adventist sanitarium where Emily worked in Chamberlain, South Dakota. (South Dakota State Historical Society)

"Do you think enough of me, Mr. Clarke, to help me once more?" she pleaded on a postcard.

In keeping with his character, Reverend Clarke promptly sent her five dollars to buy the books. He later made the following entry in his journal regarding this event:

> "Arriving there, she found that she was not old enough, and had not enough education. She sent to me for help, and I sent her money. She was studying to become a nurse. I sent her five dollars to buy books with, and she again started in school."

The sanitarium, as described in some old literature:

> "The Chamberlain Sanitarium—An Institution of Merit:
>
> The Chamberlain Sanitarium and Hospital is an up-to-date Medical and Surgical Institution utilizing in a scientific manner the various curative agencies included under the term "Physiological Therapeutics and Rational Therapy." It is operated on the same plan as the Battle Creek [Michigan] Institution and is the largest Sanitarium and Hospital in the Middle West. There are accommodations for 125 patients. Its successful operation over 15 years attests to its efficiency.
>
> The Sanitarium Nurses Training School is a recognized school, and nurses graduating from it are eligible to registration in any state. Of the 71 nurses who have graduated from our Nurses Training Course, each one has passed the state examinations.
>
> The rates at the Sanitarium in Chamberlain are $30 in a private room, including board, room and 14 treatments per week. For medical cases $1 per day is charged for medical attention after examination, which ranges from $1 up to $10. The surgical cases in private rooms are $25 per week. In a two-bed ward it costs $20 per week and includes general nursing. Special nursing will be an additional 40 cents per hour."[2]

Emily received four dollars a week for her apprentice work, and cared for four children. She and Earl kept in touch via letters and postcards to each other. After a six-month stay at the Sanitarium, Emily was summoned back to the Courtney family. The Courtneys had written that they once again needed her help. She arrived back in Milton on December 28th, 1911. Her arrival was mentioned in the January 4th edition of the Milton Telephone newspaper:

"Miss Emily Reese came from Chamberlain, S. D. Thursday, where she has been for the past six months, and will again make her home with the family of George Courtney."

Earl and Emily picked up where they left off, and grew closer and closer over the next couple months. Everything finally seemed to be going well in Emily's life. However, this soon changed. To her horror, she learned that the Courtneys could no longer keep her. It seems they just didn't need an extra set of hands anymore. Emily had scarcely been back from South Dakota two months, and now she would have to return there to her lonesome job as a Chambermaid. She was beside herself.

It was soon Sunday evening and time for church at Sandy Sink. The quaint little church was built in 1870 and dedicated the same year. It was constructed of wood, painted white, and sat atop a foundation of local fieldstones. It was attached to the Lima, Wisconsin circuit until 1886. Lima was located just a few miles east of Milton. Sandy Sink was later detached from the Lima circuit and thereafter called Otterbein station.[3]

The circuit-riding minister who served the church at the time Earl and Emily attended was the aforementioned Reverend Roberts. It was always quite late in the day by the time he made his way from the other churches to Sandy Sink, which was at the end of his circuit.

There were three rows of pews that held the approximately thirty patrons who usually attended from the nearby countryside. A large organ stood on the east end of the church, near the pulpit, which was on a raised platform. A long wooden buggy shed was located behind the church, to the east.

Reverend Charles J. Roberts is seen here on the right, along with a friend, Reverend Smelsher. This photo was taken in Wisconsin. (Ellen J. Froelich)

Two large round oak stoves heated the church. Earl's father often supplied much of the wood, and over the years it was commonplace for the ministers who served the church to spend the night with Earl's parents before returning home the next day.

As Reverend Roberts arose to begin his sermon that evening, he was surprised to see that there were only two members of the congregation present! As it turned out, due to the inclement weather, Earl was the only person to attend service from the north, and Emily was the only one that came from the south.

The Reverend proceeded with his sermon nonetheless. After all, he traveled some distance to do so, and he took his calling quite seriously. By the time the sermon was over it had become pitch black outside. There was no moon to illuminate the night sky—it was in the dead of winter. You could scarcely see your hand in front of your face.

Emily was fearful of the long walk home in the dark. She turned to Earl and said, "Oh Earl, could you please walk me home? It's so very dark out."

"Sure I can," Earl replied. As they walked down the lane in the direction of the Courtney home, Emily began to cry.

"Why, what on earth is wrong Emily?"

"Oh, Earl, I have to go back to South Dakota to work at the sanitarium and I don't know what to do. All I do is cook, clean, and dump pots for four dollars a week. It's barely enough to buy my clothes, and I have no friends there."

Earl pondered for a while, and then said, "Gosh, I don't know what I can do to help." Emily continued to cry.

"Can't you please think of something Earl?"

"Oh Earl, can't you please think of something?" begged Emily.

Earl thought for a while as they walked, unsure of what to say, and then made a startling, yet fantastic suggestion.

"Well, I guess the only thing I can do would be to marry ya."

"I'll never forget it," Earl would later recall. "She threw her arms around my neck and jumped off the ground, yellin', "Oh, Will ya? Will ya?, Will ya?"

To Emily, the dark night somehow seemed much brighter now. Earl had proposed, perhaps not on his knees, or in the traditional sense, but that didn't matter. The journey to South Dakota could be cancelled!

Emily quickly mailed a postcard to Reverend Clarke telling him of her engagement. He was in charge of the Children's Home of Cincinnati, Ohio, at the time. He made a practice of keeping in touch with the numerous children he placed over the years, so Emily was aware of his location. He later wrote in his journals that he received over 2,000 letters from his former wards every year, and endeavored to answer each one of them.

Emily's postcard was postmarked at Janesville, Wisconsin, March 8th, 1912. It read as follows:

"Dear friend,

Received your last letter some time ago will answer soon. I thought I would let you know that I am expected to be married

Sandy Sink (Otterbein United Brethren) Church that Earl and Emily Kidder attended. Note the buggy shed in the background. (Clifford Stark)

the 27th of this mo[nth] to Mr. Earl Kidder of course you will be surprise[d].

Emily Reese."

Earl's father accompanied him to the county courthouse in Janesville to obtain a marriage license. Janesville was located about eight miles to the south-southeast. Upon his arrival, Howard W. Lee, the county clerk, looked at Earl and asked very matter-of-factly:

"Young man, do you know what you're getting into? It's easy to get into, but it's darn hard to get out of it!" Earl's father chuckled, and Earl, being painfully shy, just looked at him and grinned. Lee then presented Earl with marriage license number 53.

Mr. Lee wasn't the only one to give Earl advice on marriage. John Briggs stopped by one day shortly thereafter when Earl was helping out a neighboring farmer, Alec Paul. Briggs was an African-American man that owned Briggs' Resort on Lake Koshkonong—a few miles to the northeast of Earl's home. He heard Earl was getting married and he said to

Postcard mailed to Reverend H. D. Clarke announcing Emily's plans to marry Earl Kidder. The front of the postcard featured a photo of Emily. (Courtesy of Richard Clarke)

him: "Earl, do you know if you get married, your wife can throw your money out the back door with a tablespoon faster than you can throw it in the front door with a scoop shovel?" Earl always got quite a kick out of telling that story.

On Wednesday morning, March 20, 1912—the day they were to be wed, Earl and Emily awoke to a

A picture postcard of Emily Reese when "of age". This is the front of the postcard above. (Courtesy of Richard Clarke)

terrible snowstorm. Nonetheless, Earl, Emily, and Earl's folks all climbed in the bobsled and headed for the Richards Memorial United Brethren Church in Janesville. The church stood in the northwest corner of the intersection of Prospect (now Centerway) and Milton Avenues, having been built just a few years prior.

As they approached Janesville they observed that several streetcars were stuck in the deep snow.

Upon their arrival at the church, Reverend Roberts expressed his concern about the need of two witnesses who were not family members for the wedding. Few people had ventured out in the inclement weather, but he found one in the form of a woman named Mrs. Dela Fairfield who happened to be walking down the sidewalk in front of the church, and it was decided that the other would have to be the Reverend's wife, Leona Roberts.

Mrs. Courtney sewed Emily's dress by hand from material purchased at Bostwick's on South Main Street in Janesville, and Earl bought his first suit for the occasion at Seeger's clothing store in Milton Junction. "Our friend, Alec Paul, loaned us fifty dollars for the wedding clothes," Earl later recalled. He added, "I was so darn scared the day of our wedding that I could barely say 'I do.'"

The Milton Telephone announced their marriage in the March 29th, 1912 edition:

> "Miss Emily Reese and Earl Kidder were united in marriage Wednesday morning, March 20, at the M. E. parsonage in Janesville. The bride has been making her home for the past two years at George Courtney's at Sandy Sink. The groom is the son of Mr. and Mrs. Clark Kidder, also of that vicinity. A wedding supper was enjoyed at the home of the groom's parents Wednesday evening."

Emily had never been happier. She was anxious to begin married life with Earl, and experience the love and stability that had eluded her for so very long.

These photos show the exterior and interior of Seeger's Clothing Store in Milton Junction, Wisconsin where Earl purchased his wedding suit. (Milton (WI) Historical Society)

The Richards Memorial United Brethren Church in Janesville, Wisconsin. Earl and Emily Kidder were married here by Reverend Charles J. Roberts on March 20th, 1912. (Dorothy Gunn)

The newlyweds faced the dilemma of not having a house of their own to go home to. Earl remedied the situation by erecting a twelve by fourteen foot tent in the apple orchard just south of his folks' place. It was erected atop a wooden floor, and a small stove on one end kept them warm. Earl would later comment, "There's nothin' like livin' in a tent…you just throw a newspaper in the stove now and then, and it'll keep you warm for quite a while."

Here, the young couple would spend their first two years together nestled under the limbs of the large Wolf River apple trees, planted by Earl's father decades earlier. From this meager beginning they began to build a life together.

Earl and Emily received word that Reverend Clarke was staying in nearby Albion, Wisconsin, at the home of his daughter, Mabel, so they wrote and asked him to come and pay them a visit.

It wasn't long before Reverend Clarke took them up on their invitation. After returning home from his visit, he sat down and typed up a report

The actual page in Rev. Clarke's scrapbook featuring Earl and Emily (Reese) Kidder's wedding photo and other information. (Courtesy of Mrs. Walter Sayre)

Earl and Emily with their sister-in-law, Merle (Kidder) Garthwaite. (Courtesy of the author)

```
                        Albion,Wis., Oct.22nd 1912.
Dear Mr.Brace:-I think I oncesent you for  recording in Vol.41 if wanted,
the marriage notice of Emily Reese,#3993,41/388, to Mr.Earl Kidder,of Edger-
ton.Wis.,RFD#4.     While on a short trip in Wis. and Minn., and by earnest
request of Mr.and Mrs.Kidder, I spent a day with them and find them happy.
Mr.Kidder a farmer. Married March 20th 1912.
   "Emily" wants if a possible thing,knowledge of her brother Richard Reese,
who if I mistake not is about two years older than she and was in one of
your Industrial Schools and perhaps placed out by your Society. I think he
was. She cares nothing for any others of her family but Richard. Can you
give me any clew to him ? Would be grateful if you can.

   I now go to Dodge Center,Minn. for a few days. May stay until election.
                        Sincerely,
                                    H. D. Clarke.
```

The report Reverend Clarke sent back to the Society after visiting Earl and Emily shortly after their marriage. (Children's Aid Society) to the Society regarding Earl and Emily's wedding and his recent visit to them. It reveals that Emily's longing for her birth family had at least temporarily been replaced with anger and she wanted only to get in touch with her brother, Richard. The refusal of her older siblings to rescue her and her brother Richard from the orphanage left them both extremely disappointed with them. The report is reproduced below.

Emily was about to give birth to their first child in late June, 1913 and was taken inside Earl's parents' farmhouse. She was having a great deal of trouble with the delivery, and no less than three doctors and as many nurses were called to assist. Earl later recalled the day: "You could hear her screaming a half mile away. My mother said, 'My word, is she having twins?'"

They named their first child Mildred Frances Kidder (after Emily's friend and former employer, Frances Courtney). She was born on June

Earl and Emily's son, Warren, is holding his cousin, Richard Kidder, along the path that led from Earl's folks' house to the old granary that Earl and Emily had lived in years earlier. At the time of this photo, the granary was being occupied by Earl's younger brother, Clark, his wife, Eunice, and their son, Richard, seen here. Earl and Emily had also lived in a tent under the Wolf River apple trees seen in this photo. (Mr. and Mrs. Richard Kidder)

28th, 1913. Mildred was followed by Bernice Ruth in 1914; Earl Alfred (after one of the Courtneys' sons, Alfred) in 1917; Donald Leo in 1919; Warren Owen in 1922, and Marian Emily in 1926.

After Earl and Emily had grown tired of living in a tent, Earl decided to renovate his folks' old granary into a home for them. It was moved to where the tent had been located in the orchard. When completed it consisted of a kitchen, dining room, pantry, and a bedroom. The couple soon moved into their four-room former corncrib, which truly seemed like a mansion to them after living in a tent for so long!

Their first night in the new home was quite an eventful one as Earl later recalled:

"We woke up in the middle of the night after hearing a noise. A large man was climbing in through our bedroom window! My folks used to let the hobos and bums who rode the trains sleep in one room of the granary, which had a stove and a pile of wood they could cut to burn, along with a bucksaw to cut it with. The railroad tracks ran right behind our house. They had the place marked with something that let them know it was a safe-haven, but we never did find out what it was. Anyway, I had to act quick under the circumstances, so I yelled out, 'I'll get my gun' to Emily, and boy did he go!"

Shortly after he married Emily, Earl began hoeing tobacco for a neighbor, Guv Wixom, for fifty cents a day. After he finished work late one afternoon he drove the buggy into Milton to pick up Emily, who was visiting the Courtneys. The Courtneys had moved to a farm just east of Milton.

In those days a serious illness could easily take your life. Penicillin was not yet invented, and simple pneumonia could be deadly.

On the way home Earl began to feel sick, so he and Emily decided to stop at Doc Coon's house in Milton Junction for some medicine. Emily went in and got it for him. They were about halfway home when Earl became gravely ill. He quickly learned that he had pneumonia. If he was not careful, it could take his life. The doctor was summoned immediately.

Several neighbors took turns helping Emily care for Earl. They consisted of Pearl Randolph and Lettie and Art Holmes. In addition, Earl's aunt, Eva (Kidder) Hall, and a cousin, Ada Brandt, also took turns assisting. Emily was so fearful that she was going to lose Earl and prayed daily for his recovery.

Earl lay in bed from November until April 10th of the following year. He later recalled how he literally lived on eggnog. A medicated poultice called Antiphlogestine was smeared on his chest, with a hot cloth placed over it. He shrank from 185 pounds down to 135, and his father had to carry him to the supper table each day. One day, near the end of his ordeal, Emily snuck him in one of her homemade dill pickles, and he never forgot how very good it tasted.

In the spring following Earl's recovery he went in on halves with his father on the family farm. He also began taking odd jobs in the neighborhood to earn enough money to support his growing family. He was looking forward to a bright future.

When World War I broke out, he received official notification that he would need to register for the draft. His mother kept telling him to hold off going to register for just one more day until the final day came, and he absolutely had to go.

Just as he did on the day of his wedding, he awoke that morning to a blizzard. Earl's folks had agreed to watch the children. Earl would later look back on his misfortune when it came to snowstorms and exclaim, "I learned that you never put off until tomorrow what you can do today."

Emily was wrapped in a warm blanket and they got in a bobsled to begin the trip to Janesville. They had to go to a place near the County Farm on Highway 14, about seven miles due south of their farm.

By the time they were finished in Janesville the snow was piled up to a depth of four feet, with drifts approaching ten feet high. Earl attempted to get the team of horses turned around for the trip home, but it was futile. His neighbors had somehow gotten word of his predicament, and several of them arrived in their bobsleds to help shovel a path so the team could be turned around.

Earl was put in the Grade A class for the draft, but was fortunate enough to not be called. Farmers were needed to help feed the country, and were generally the last ones to be called for duty.

Armistice was signed on November 11th, 1918. Earl was spared, but a half million other Americans were not.

Chapter Six
A Place to Call Home

"To my dying day I shall have deepest interest in the work of placing and caring for orphan or homeless children."

- Reverend H. D. Clarke

Earl and Emily decided to rent a farm consisting of 160 acres situated about a mile to the north of Earl's folks' place. The farm was owned by members of the Kidder family since the late 1840s. The owner at the time was Julia (Kidder) Roper, one of Earl's cousins. Realizing that they did not have the money required to rent the farm, Earl and Emily decided to pay a visit to a neighbor and friend of the family, John Hurd. Hurd owned several hundred acres a few miles to the northwest toward Edgerton. He was a robust, rough-talking man. He invited Earl and Emily in, and after chatting briefly, Earl explained his predicament. John roared back with "Why the hell didn't you marry a big fat dutch girl like your brother Bill did—someone to help with farm work—instead of such a scrawny little thing!" Emily slid behind Earl and began tugging on the back of his shirt, pleading, "Let's go Earl, Let's go Earl." Earl thanked John for his time and as he and Emily turned to walk out the door, John asked, "Where are you going? You aren't going to leave without your money, are you?" Earl and Emily were in the farming business.

It was at this farm that Earl and Emily's children would all be reared, except for their first born, Mildred. Times were tough and Earl and Emily were struggling to keep all of their children fed. It was decided that Earl's parents, Clark and Elma, would take in Mildred who was seven years old at the time. The close proximity of the two farms allowed for very frequent visits.

Earl and Emily received another visit from Reverend Clarke at their new home. He was in the area visiting his daughter Mabel Sayre and her family in Albion, about six miles to the north. He learned of Emily's whereabouts and decided to pay a visit. Earl and Emily introduced him to their children and they spent several hours visiting. As Reverend Clarke drove away, Emily couldn't help but recall all those times that he had come to replace her in years past. All those prior homes had led her to the one she had now—a lasting and loving one. How comforting it must have been to Reverend Clarke as well, to finally see Emily happy, and surrounded by love.

Earl and Emily both enjoyed celebrating holidays with their children. Christmas was always a special time of year for them. About a week before Christmas, Earl would cut a Christmas tree locally. Earl, as well as many of the locals, often obtained their trees from a grove that grew just to the south, near Sandy Sink. The trees were too large to bring the entire tree home, so they simply cut the tops off!

Every Christmas Eve the children would assist Earl and Emily with the making of homemade ice cream and molasses popcorn balls (see Appendix V for recipes). They would have a taffy pull with the excess molasses syrup used to bind the popcorn balls. It was heated and then poured into a dip pan and allowed to harden a little. It was then pulled into long round rolls until it turned yellowish-white in color, and was quickly cut into small pieces while it was still soft. The children would string popcorn and cranberries to decorate the tree.

One Christmas money was in very short supply, so Earl and Emily dressed several ducks to sell to raise the money to buy gifts for the children. When the time came, the snow was so deep that neither horse nor car could make it through to Edgerton so Earl could purchase the gifts. Earl knew the railroad tracks would be clear so he headed out on foot with a gunnysack full of the dressed ducks, and made the long trek to Edgerton to sell them to townspeople, who would undoubtedly serve them for Christmas dinner. Earl returned with gifts for them all that year, which included a pair of skis for each child.

A very special treat would await the children in their stockings on Christmas morning—a sweet juicy orange. Oranges were very expensive in those days, and many families could only afford them on special occasions. The same was true of bananas—Earl would often have to purchase them when overripe and on sale. Bags of candy kisses were also placed in the stockings.

Emily made sure that each Christmas was a memorable one, unlike all the uneventful Christmases that came and went while she was in the orphanage. Oh, there were plenty of other children around then, but she still had an overwhelming feeling of being alone. The impersonal and regimented atmosphere in the orphanage could not compare to a Christmas spent with one's family.

One other holiday became a particularly memorable one for the family as well, but not in the way they would have liked.

The Fourth of July was fast approaching one summer and Earl had purchased twenty-five dollars' worth of fireworks to light off for the people in the neighborhood. A wooden chute was erected over the gravel pit at his folks' house for that purpose. He stored the fireworks in a back room at their farmhouse.

One day Emily decided she would give their two girls, Mildred and Bernice, a little preview and removed one of the sparklers from its box. She lit it and as she was heading out of the room with it, a single spark found its way inside one of the boxes that held some of the larger fireworks. All of a sudden, the whole works was set ablaze! Skyrockets and Roman candles were flying everywhere and bounced off the walls of the nearby kitchen. The curtains quickly caught fire.

Emily grabbed a girl in each arm and took off running. Earl heard the commotion and came running just in time to see Emily struck in the rear end with a skyrocket! Luckily he was able to douse the fire before too much damage was done, though it took some time before the foul odor was gone in the house. He always got quite a charge out of relating the story of Emily's close encounter with the skyrocket to friends and family.

Though farm life had its share of hardships, there were lighter times as well. In one such instance, Earl and Emily decided to purchase a horse from their friend, Jim Van Etta. Jim was always "full of the devil," as Earl later recalled. It so happened that he had wanted to purchase some hogs, and Earl had a half-dozen that ate chickens. He and Jim agreed to a trade, and Earl sent his hired had over to Jim's house to retrieve the horse, sight unseen. Little did Earl and Emily know that the horse they had just traded for was a former racehorse!

One day Emily had their hired hand, whose nickname was "Duck," hitch the horse up for her so that she could head into Milton Junction to sell several dozen eggs to the store. She got about halfway to town when she noticed the horse was galloping awfully fast. Naturally, she began to pull back on the reins to slow the horse down. Well, to a racehorse, this was a signal to go faster! Emily panicked and pulled harder and harder on the reins, causing the horse to run faster and faster.

A farmer happened to spot the runaway horse and buggy coming up the road and quickly mounted his horse. He waited for Emily to approach and eventually caught up with Emily's buggy. He latched onto the horse and was able to stop it. Earl and Emily thought it was just a freak incident and decided to keep the horse.

About a week later, Emily decided to call on the Courtneys at their home just east of Milton. She loaded Earl Junior, who was just a baby, into the buggy. She thought it best to hold him on her lap as they rode along. Again, when about halfway into town, the horse began to pick up speed. And again, Emily panicked. The buggy swerved dangerously from side to side as the wheels caught the deep ruts that were left in the road after a recent rain, now rock hard after drying in the hot sun. As Emily approached a bend the buggy left the edge of the road and the right wheel struck a tree stump with such force that it threw her and the baby high into the air! She lit squarely on her hind end, with Earl Junior still in her lap. Amazingly, neither of them were hurt.

Earl and Emily seriously discussed selling the horse after this second incident, but they knew that they had no money to purchase another one, and no livestock to trade for one. They decided to just be very careful with the horse from then on, and not pull too hard on the reins again!

One day, they decided they would take all the kids to Newville to purchase some apples and fresh cider. Newville was a tiny hamlet situated on the north bank of the Rock River, about two miles to the northeast of their farm.

The family made it to Newville safely and were nearly back home when the horse's gait grew faster and faster. Earl's attempts to slow the animal down were futile, and just as they approached the driveway to their farm, the horse and two wheels broke away from the buggy. Everyone flew forward as the front of the buggy dug deep into the soil below.

Again, very fortunately, no one was seriously injured. This time they had enough though. They decided to give the horse to their hired hand, Duck, but they coyly decided not to tell him about the fact that it was a racehorse.

One day the horse ran away from Duck and headed directly up the railroad tracks. A train was coming down the tracks some distance away and the engineer spotted the horse coming at breakneck speed. He grabbed one of the scoop shovels used to shovel coal, and just as the horse came by, he leaned out of the train and struck the horse on the head with enough force to stop it in its tracks!

It wasn't long after these episodes with the racehorse that Earl and Emily decided it was high time they bought themselves one of those horseless carriages that were all the rage. The cost of a Model T Ford at the time was a whopping one hundred and forty dollars. In order to buy the car, they raised a large flock of tame Black Spanish turkeys and sold them to Harold Van Galder, a Janesville tavern owner.

The car was purchased at Prelep's on North Main Street in Janesville. Earl later recalled, "The car used to kick every time I cranked it." The days of the run-away racehorses were over!

One day, Emily proclaimed that she wanted to learn how to drive their new car. Though a little apprehensive, Earl obliged. After a few minutes of instructions, Emily got behind the wheel. Earl crank started the car. Emily took a deep breath as she put the car in gear. She insisted that Earl not ride along. She wanted to do this by herself. She let off the clutch too quickly and the car leaped forward with a sudden jerk, which killed the engine. Earl told her to let up on the clutch a little easier the next time, and he restarted the car.

Earl instructed Emily to head east down one of the farm lanes and into a field of corn that had just been picked. There was but one tree near the center of the field, and as Earl stood watching, he joked with the hired hand that Emily would probably hit it.

Meanwhile, Emily was feeling quite confident and applied more gas. As she approached the tree, she tried in vain to turn the wheel to the right so that she would avoid striking it. The front wheels began to slide on the slippery stalks of corn underneath, and she panicked. By the time she applied the brakes the car was too close to the tree and slammed right into it! Luckily, the only thing that was injured was her pride and the car's front bumper. Earl and the hired hand quickly came running to her rescue, relieved to see that she was okay. She then had some explaining to do to Earl. She never did attempt to drive again.

Earl could be quite the prankster. One spring day, he and Emily decided to head down to the Kidder shanty on the Rock River and go for a boat ride. Earl's father built the shanty in the 1860s when he was a teenager. It was the first such shanty for a very long stretch of the Rock River west of Newville. The shanty was nestled amongst a stand of large Butternut trees, very near the water's edge.

Upon their arrival, Earl walked over to a large willow tree that protruded out over the water some distance. He knew from past experience that water snakes would often slither out onto the limbs to sun themselves after emerging from their winter hibernation. Sure enough, the limbs were full of dozens of Spotted Adder and various kinds of water snakes indigenous to the area. Emily was in the shanty and he didn't tell her.

Every time Earl entered the shanty he would recall the time that he and his sister Leta spent the night there when they were youngsters. The shanty consisted of just two rooms, one of which was a bedroom. A two-by-four was nailed to the wall above the two small beds. When Earl woke up the next morning he found himself face to face with a five-foot long Spotted Adder snake, stretched out on the top of the two-by-four! "He lay there spitting at me," he would later recall. He added, "I never slept very well there again."

He walked to the shanty and asked Emily if she was ready to go for their boat ride. She was. Earl slowly rowed the boat over underneath the limbs of the willow tree, which hung just six feet or so above the water. He positioned himself directly under the limb that held the snakes, and told Emily to look up. He knew she was deathly afraid of snakes. When she looked up, she let out a scream and flew to the other end of the boat, clinging tightly to Earl. The boat nearly tipped over!

It didn't take Earl long to row out from under the tree as he didn't like snakes any better than Emily did, and feared the commotion would cause the snakes to drop out of the trees on top of them! Emily promptly cancelled the rest of the boat trip, and did not speak to Earl for some time afterwards.

Chapter Seven

Reunions and Farewells

"They will remember him, who turned the tides of their lives for the better, and for eternity."

—Reverend H.D. Clarke

Emily received a most unexpected letter in the mail one day. It was from her brother Lewis Reese, Junior, in New York City! He somehow managed to find her, and he and his wife wanted to come out to visit Emily and her family. They would also stop and pick up their sister Jane on the way, who happened to live in Chicago. Emily was excited and nervous at the same time. She wrote them back immediately and told them they were most welcome to visit.

On the day they arrived they made their way up the long and narrow gravel driveway at the farm in a big fancy car. Emily and Bernice greeted them at the front porch. Lewis proclaimed, "Why, which one is the mother and which is the daughter?" Emily still looked very young for her age.

They had a joyous reunion, but it was tempered by the news that Emily's father had died of cancer in 1912, and her mother's whereabouts was unknown. Most heartbreaking of all for Emily was when her brother Lewis told her of finding their brother Richard at his home on Long Island. He had joined the Army and attained the rank of Lieutenant. It seems that, like Emily, he became so disenchanted about his experiences as a child that he wanted nothing more to do with the family; though he felt no ill will towards Emily.

As Lewis was leaving, he gave her a postcard photo of Richard in uniform—a keepsake Richard sent along for Emily. Emily was devastated when Lewis related the story to her and presented her with the photograph. Tears filled her eyes, and her heart sank. The photograph and the fleeting glimpses of Richard that she had in the Home for Destitute Children would have to last her a lifetime. To her dying day, Emily lamented over never seeing Richard again, always wondering how he made out in life and dreaming of their reunion.

Seeing her brother Lewis and sister Jane made Emily long to be reunited with her other brothers and sisters. Earl encouraged her to go and visit them. Money was tight, but by 1927, she had saved up enough for the long-awaited trip back to the place where her life began so precariously—Brooklyn. She went to meet the brothers and sisters she never really knew, with the sad exception of Richard.

This train ride would be far different than the one she took nearly thirty years earlier. It held promise, and a chance to connect with siblings—with family. She stayed for two weeks, learning about her roots and getting to know her long-lost siblings, as well as her nieces and nephews. During research on this book her niece Clara (Reese) Pluskat would reveal to me nearly seventy years later that it was on this trip that Emily confided in them that she was indeed assaulted at one of the foster homes in Iowa.

In the years ensuing, Emily's brother Lewis visited one other time, and her sister Jane, along with her husband Bill, came to visit fairly often from Chicago.

Emily corresponded with her brothers and sisters in New York for many years, but would never see any of them again. The deep

A postcard photo of Lieutenant Richard Reese, given to Emily as a keepsake. (Courtesy of the author)

bonds that normally form between brothers and sisters never had a chance to do so between Emily and her siblings. After all, Emily barely knew them. She never did learn the fate of her dear mother.

When family and friends would quiz Emily about the circumstances that led to her placement in an orphanage, she would declare that both of her parents had died of pneumonia, leaving her orphaned. The truth was just too painful for her to reveal.

It was just a few days after Christmas in 1928 when Earl and Emily received the sad news that Reverend Clarke passed away on Christmas Day at the Edgerton Hospital from kidney failure. He was seventy-eight years old.

His final years were spent with his daughter Mabel (Clarke) Sayre and her family in Albion, just north of Edgerton. Earl and Emily were very saddened by the news. His obituary read, in part:

> "Elder Clarke was a man of strong convictions, deep feeling, and unswerving loyalty to his ideals. He was a loyal friend, a loving husband, and a patient, tender father. He had spent his final years at the home of his daughter Mabel in Albion, Wisconsin, spending much of his time corresponding with many of his former wards who looked to him for counsel and encouragement, and in whom he remained interested to the last."

He was laid to rest beside his wife, Anna, in Dodge Center, Minnesota. Anna died in 1912 during his tenure at the Children's Country Homes Society of Cincinnati.

By his own estimation, he placed nearly 1,200 children in homes during his employment with the Children's Aid Society, The Children's Home Society of Cincinnati, Ohio, and the Haskell Home in Battle Creek, Michigan. One of the last entries he made in his journal was this:

"To my dying day I shall have deepest interest in the work of placing and caring for orphan or homeless children. Some dear friends say it was the greatest work of my life. The God of the orphan is the judge of that. The work has brought me greatest happiness, and in a few cases, great grief and misunderstanding, or rather disappointment. The thousands of letters from them and their homes all these years testify to the success of it, and to their appreciation, in so many cases. They will remember him, who turned the tides of their lives for the better, and for eternity.

Reverend H. D. Clarke holding his granddaughter, Dorthea, in 1928. (Courtesy of Mrs. Walter Sayre)

If God in His mercy shall give me a place in heaven, I hope to see among the redeemed, many of these souls who were snatched from poverty and woe, and given a home with advantages on earth, and grew up respectable citizens."

On May 31st, 1929, just months after the death of Reverend Clarke, the Children's Aid Society sent a group of children to the town of Sulphur Springs, Texas on what is generally considered to be the last documented orphan train in America.[1]

Earl was an avid hunter and each fall he would make the trip to the north woods of Wisconsin during deer season. Emily rarely accompanied Earl on these trips, but Earl's folks agreed to watch the children one year and Emily decided to ride along.

It was during the height of Prohibition and one of Earl's friends convinced Earl to let him bring a jug of moonshine along on the trip. In those days it was customary to bring a jug of kerosene along to clean the snow and ice off the windshield of the car as there was no such thing as windshield wipers or washing fluid. Earl's friend, whose name also happened to be Earl, decided that he would put the moonshine in a jug exactly like the one used to carry the kerosene so as to conceal it.

They decided to stop for dinner at Wisconsin Rapids along the way and just as they pulled up in front of a restaurant, a big burly policeman came walking over to their car to greet them. The two jugs were wrapped in a blanket under Earl's friends' feet, and when he went to step out of the car to greet the policeman his shoe became entangled in the blanket, causing one of the jugs to roll out on the ground. It came to a rest against the policeman's boots. The two Earls held their breath as the policeman bent over and picked the jug up. They had no idea if the jug that rolled out was the one that held the moonshine or the kerosene. The policeman popped off the cork and proceeded to smell the contents. To their extreme delight he exclaimed, "Well, that's all right boys, it's kerosene. You have a good day now folks."

As the policeman walked away, Emily commented to the two Earls, "Why, who would be dumb enough to be transporting moonshine these days anyway, there's a thousand dollar fine if you're caught." The Earls answered in unison, "That's right, Emily." It was not until much later that Emily learned the truth.

Life on the farm was trying in those days, to say the least. A severe drought began its deadly grip on the Midwest and southern plains in 1931. Along with it came the Great Depression. As crops began to die, so began the "black blizzards," created by blowing dust from the withered fields, the over-plowed and over-grazed land. Fourteen such dust storms occurred in 1932. The following year, no less than thirty-eight such storms smothered the unfortunate inhabitants of the afflicted areas.

By 1934, more than seventy-five percent of the country was affected by the drought, with twenty-seven states reporting severe conditions. It was reported that the dry winds had blown away and otherwise eroded 35 million acres of formerly cultivated land, with an additional 225 million acres of cultivated land losing topsoil at a rapid rate. The infamous "Black Sunday" occurred on April 14th, 1935, aptly named for the worst "Black Blizzard" of the Dust Bowl. It was not until 1939 that the rains finally returned, and the Great Depression slowly began to subside.

In the middle of it all, Earl and Emily, like so many others, were in dire straits. They were no longer able to keep up the mortgage payments on their farm and faced a similar fate to that of so many families. They received word that their farm would be sold on the steps of the county courthouse.

As they anguished over the situation, Earl decided to go see his good friend, Fred McIntyre, who dealt in tobacco in Edgerton and was active in the bank. Earl explained his situation and Fred graciously agreed to advance Earl ten thousand dollars so that he could attend the auction and perhaps have a chance to buy the farm back. Earl had sold Mr. McIntyre his tobacco crop for many years.

Word got out that a wealthy attorney from Janesville had decided that he wanted the farm and would be attending the auction. One of Earl and Emily's neighbors also wanted it, but he told them that he would not bid against Earl if he had his heart set on keeping the farm. Mr. McIntyre instructed Earl to go to the bank on the morning of the sale and he would leave word for the tellers to allow Earl to withdraw the money.

When Earl arrived that morning he observed a fellow farmer talking to one of the bank officers. He was attempting to borrow enough money to save his farm from a similar fate. He was refused, and when he got up to leave he slowly backed up against the wall, slumped to the floor, and cried like a child—a sight Earl would never forget. Earl realized just how lucky he and Emily were that day.

When the day of the auction came, Earl and Emily dropped the children off at Earl's folks' house and headed to the courthouse in Janesville. When they arrived they quickly spotted the attorney who planned on bidding for the farm among the small group of people who congregated on the steps of the courthouse. The auctioneer stepped forward and proclaimed, "Okay, we're here to sell the Earl and Emily Kidder farm in Edgerton." People looked over at Earl and Emily with curiosity, and pity.

"I'll bid seven thousand dollars," shouted the attorney.

The auctioneer replied, "Do I have any other bids?"

The crowd was silent.

"I'll bid seventy-five hundred," Earl calmly said.

With that, the crowd's curiosity turned to astonishment, for they wondered where on earth Earl and Emily came up with the money in such times. The attorney thought he would surely not have to pay a penny more than seven thousand and was quite taken aback when Earl topped his bid by five hundred dollars. He pondered for a moment, and then turned and walked away.

"Do I have any other bids?" asked the auctioneer.

The crowd was silent. Earl reached down and held Emily's hand firmly. They both held their breath. "SOLD!" shouted the auctioneer. Earl and Emily embraced each other as they were overwhelmed with relief.

Things were still very difficult, of course. There was little or no money to buy food for the family, and before long, they were forced to take several of their Plymouth Rock chickens to trade for five dollars' worth of groceries at a store in Milton Junction.

Upon their arrival the store owner was sympathetic, but he told Earl that he couldn't accept any more chickens in trade as he was inundated with such requests.

It so happened that a gentleman named Tony Lukas was in the store at the time and overheard Earl's conversation. He stepped forward and insisted on paying for Earl's groceries. Earl had never met the man before. The two became lifelong friends after that and went on many hunting trips together in the north woods of Wisconsin.

As if the searing heat of the 1930s had not caused enough devastation in Earl and Emily's life, it was about to add insult to injury. Earl and Emily decided to head to town to run some errands one hot summer day. While they were gone their herd of purebred sheep consumed the last of the their available water. Desperate to find more, they all gathered and pushed against the gate to their pen, causing the latch to break.

As they ran freely in the yard they spied a tank full of fuel oil that sat near the farmhouse. The spout on the end of the tank resembled the end of the hose that supplied water to the tank in their pen. They began to chew on it, and suddenly the lever was switched on. The fuel oil spilled all over the ground and pooled in a shallow depression. The unsuspecting sheep, in their dire thirst, lapped up every last drop that spilled out.

Earl and Emily returned home later and as they drove up the long driveway to the farmhouse, they were overcome by the horror that lay before them. Dozens of sheep lay dead, strewn across the yard and up the driveway. It was a costly and devastating loss.

It was on another hot summer day in the 1930s that Earl and Emily noticed the sky getting darker and darker. It became nearly as dark as night. To the west, near the river, Earl could see what he thought were trees blowing around high up in the sky. He realized that a tornado was bearing down on them. He told Emily and the children to get down into the cellar immediately. He quickly locked up as many doors as he could and headed for the house.

As he ran he witnessed a large bundle of wheat shocks in one of his nearby fields being lifted straight up nearly three hundred feet into the air. He turned to see the steel wheel of his windmill being blown off and watched it land right in the middle of his herd of purebred Ayreshire cows who had huddled nervously in the barnyard. Amazingly not one of them was injured. As he was going into the basement the roof was blown off the west end of the farmhouse.

After the tornado passed, they all emerged from the basement. Earl found that their Model T Ford had been blown from its position in front of the house clear down into a cornfield to the east. The barn, which Earl had built himself, was shaken so badly that the tobacco poles fell from the rafters inside. It later required several steel rods to stabilize it. Earl and Emily were shocked when they observed a supple piece of straw that was deeply imbedded in the trunk of a nearby tree.

Earl and Emily pose with their daughter, Marian, on right, and son, Earl, Jr. in this circa 1930s photo taken in front of their farmhouse on Kidder Road. (Couresy of the author)

Several neighbors fared much worse than Earl and Emily, losing much more in the way of buildings and livestock. Fortunately, no lives were lost as they were in the last big tornado that had struck Milton and Milton Junction on November 11, 1911.

In 1935, Earl was made Town Constable by Rock County Sheriff, Jimmy Croak. He was hired "to clean up Indian Ford," as the town had "gone wild." Indian Ford marked a place south of Edgerton, where Indians and earlier settlers frequently crossed the Rock River. It was located in Fulton Township. He served as Constable for Milton and Fulton Townships, a job that he would have for nearly forty years.

That same year Emily was pregnant with her seventh child. On July 21st, while visiting at Earl's folks' house, she was standing near some pine trees on the north side of the farmhouse when a car full of teenagers came barreling down Kidder Road. They lost control of their car and struck a large boulder that was embedded in a small patch of wild plum bushes in the ditch.

Earl and his brother Bill had dynamited that very boulder out of the way when Kidder Road was constructed years earlier. The road ran just east of the farmhouse. The force of the crash sent one of the young boys through the front windshield, severely cutting his head. Emily witnessed the whole event and began screaming and running for help.

Earl's mother, Elma, assisted Emily to the bedroom where she could be calmed down. She was exhausted and fell asleep. When she awoke the next morning, she could no longer feel the baby kicking, and Earl quickly rushed her to the hospital in Edgerton. Hours later, their baby boy was still born.

Earl later recalled the event: "He was a beautiful baby. He had a head full of jet-black hair. We named him Kenneth."

When Earl arrived at the hospital the next day the nurse proclaimed, "Why, you're just in time Mr. Kidder. Would you like to see your child one last time?"

"What do you mean?" quizzed Earl.

"Why, I was just heading to the incinerator with him," she replied.

Earl did not know that it was the hospital's policy to place such babies in the incinerator. "Why, you won't do any such thing!" Earl exclaimed. "I'm taking my baby and giving him a proper burial!"

And so he did.

Earl consulted with a local undertaker who agreed to supply a baby casket and handle the arrangements for one hundred dollars. As a stipulation, Earl would have to help dig the grave. A service was held at the grave the following day, and the child was laid to rest alongside Earl's

The tent Earl and Emily erected at the Parker estate. Don Kidder, on right. (Courtesy of the author)

Earl and Emily pose in front of the two cottages that Earl built at the Ken Parker estate. (Courtesy of Marian Boughton)

grandfather, Joseph Cromwell Kidder, at the crest of little knoll in Edgerton's Fassett cemetery. Earl and Emily faithfully decorated the grave each Memorial Day for the rest of their lives.

After living nearly twenty-five years on the farm on Kidder Road, the farm was purchased from Earl and Emily by their son, Earl Junior (known as Bub) and his wife Louise. Earl and Emily moved to the Kenneth Parker

```
                    WESTERN              1202
CLASS OF SERVICE                                SYMBOLS
                                                DL = Day Letter
                     UNION                      NT = Overnight Telegram
                                                LC = Deferred Cable
                                                NLT = Cable Night Letter
                                                Ship Radiogram
```

NUMBER	RECEIVED AT	CHECK
	RA 39 GOVT	

Dated WUX AAB BLYTZ CALIF 759PM SEPT 23

To EARL KIDDER
    ROUTE 1
    MILTON JCT, WIS.

REGRET TO INFORM YOU FLIGHT OFFICER DONALD L. KIDDER FATALLY INJURED IN AIRCRAFT ACCIDENT WHICH OCCURRED AT 1100PM SEPT 22 AT WALDO KANSAS PERIOD REQUEST DISPOSITION OF REMAINS PERIOD ALL ARRANGEMENTS WILL BE MADE AT THIS HEADQUARTERS.

Col. CARMACK COMMANDING 34TH BOMB GP 1117P

Western Union Telegram with the news of Donald L. Kidder's death.
(Courtesy of Marian Boughton)

estate on Vogel Road, just a few miles to the northeast, where Earl was offered a job as caretaker. It was 1937. Parker, his boss, was owner of the famous Parker Pen Company located in Janesville, Wisconsin.

Once again, Earl and Emily resided in a tent—it featured wood floors and two rooms! The arrangement was temporary, as before, until Earl could erect a home and two cottages. One of his duties as caretaker was to plant thousands of pine trees on the property, as well as a host of apple, peach and pear trees. He also cared for hundreds of mink for Mr. Parker and built ponds. This job would last eight years. Earl would later declare that they were "the best years of my life." He and Emily developed a lifelong friendship with Mr. and Mrs. Parker, and at one time, Parker offered Earl and Emily a gift of a hundred acre farm and ten thousand dollars in the bank. Earl refused the offer. He believed that you had to earn what you got in life.

Lieutenant Donald L. Kidder, 1919-1943. (Courtesy of the author)

Tragedy struck on the September 22, 1943. A telegram arrived telling Earl and Emily that their son Donald was killed in a plane crash near Waldo, Kansas.

Don and ten other servicemen were ferrying a B-24 Liberator Bomber to Texas from their base in Blythe, California. They changed course to avoid an electrical storm and then became disoriented in the dust being blown around by the strong winds associated with the storm. At about 11:00 p.m. they found themselves barely clearing the tops of trees when they suddenly spotted a large hill about 2,000 feet ahead of them. They turned the plane sharply to the right to avoid collision, but the right wing of the plane dug deep into the Kansas prairie. The plane somersaulted and burst into a ball of flames, killing everyone aboard.

Earl knew that Mildred was teaching at the North Milton School, so he took off to tell her the news. Mildred later recalled that day:

"Dad came into the room holding his hat. His face was as white as a ghost. I knew something was terribly wrong."

When the casket arrived, Earl reluctantly opened it at the urging of a couple of friends, only to discover that there was nothing more than bloodstained soil inside. He would forever regret his decision to look inside. Don was laid to rest in the family plot in Milton East Cemetery. His death left a large void in the hearts of all who knew him. He was a very outgoing and likeable young man, having graduated with honors from the Milton High School. Earl and Emily now had a second child's grave to decorate every year. They were never quite the same after Don's death.

Chapter Eight

A Final Home for Emily

> *"Emily and Earl Dane Kidder, of Milton, Wisconsin, are celebrating seventy-one years...on their way to forever together."*
>
> —Radio personality Paul Harvey

In the spring of 1946, Earl and Emily were presented with the opportunity to buy a 174-acre farm owned by a man named Johnny Paul. It was located just a couple miles southwest of the Kenneth Parker estate, at the intersection of County Road N and Highway 59.

They decided to go ahead and buy it, and they were soon farming once again. They raised melons and other vegetables, which they sold at their roadside stand. This little stand later evolved into the Kidder Farm Market, a family business that would last the next 55 years. Earl and Emily also raised a large flock of chickens and sold eggs to local customers and restaurants. They raised hogs and cattle and cared for a large orchard on the farm. Earl continued with his job as Town Constable until the early 1970s. There was no problem staying busy. They would live out the rest of their lives at this farm.

The farm that Earl and Emily purchased in 1946 on County Road N in Milton Township. They operated it with their son Warren, who joined them in 1948. (Courtesy of the author)

Earl and Emily pose in 1951 on the front yard of their farm on County Road N, Milton. Emily is front center holding a baby and Earl is in front on right holding his hat. (Courtesy of Mildred (Kidder) Yahnke)

Earl and Emily posed for this photo in March 1962 on the occasion of their 50th wedding anniversary in the living room of their farmhouse in Milton, Wisconsin with four of their five surviving children stand behind them. Left to right: Earl, Jr., Bernice, Marian, and Warren. Their daughter, Mildred, was ill at the time.
(Courtesy of the author)

When it came time to apply for Social Security, Emily wrote to New York to obtain a copy of her birth certificate, which was required by the Social Security Administration. When it arrived Emily was very surprised to learn that she was actually a year older than she thought she was, and had been celebrating her birthday on the wrong day for decades! The certificate revealed her actual day of birth was the 28th of March, not the 27th! It was one of those details that were so often lost in the sketchy lives of orphans.

As the golden years encroached and then passed by, Earl and Emily developed many health problems. Earl was diagnosed with colon cancer in the late 1960s, but doctors were able to remove it all.

Earl and Emily's numerous grandchildren, great grandchildren, and great-great grandchildren brought much happiness to them during this time in their lives, and certainly helped keep them both young. Emily would keep track of all of their birthdays and would always send each one

Earl and Emily Kidder in 1973, holding Robbie Hill—one of their several great-grandchildren. (Courtesy of the author)

Author Clark Kidder poses with his grandparents, Earl and Emily, at their Milton farmhouse on the occasion of their 63rd wedding anniversary in March 1975. (Courtesy of the author)

a card with a couple dollars in it. She knew, perhaps more than anyone, just how precious a family was.

Earl made a daily ritual of going to the Squeeze Inn restaurant in Milton Junction each morning to share coffee and conversation with friends and townspeople.

In 1983, on the occasion of their 71st wedding anniversary, U. S. Representative John Manske, a native of Milton, arranged for the State Assembly of Wisconsin to issue a Citation to Earl and Emily in honor of their longstanding service to the community and government in the Milton area.

U. S. Representative John Manske presents Earl and Emily with a Citation from the Assembly of the State of Wisconsin in 1983 on the occasion of their 71st Wedding Anniversary. Emily had recently broken her wrist in a fall at their farm home.
(Courtesy of the author)

The Citation by the Wisconsin State Assembly that was presented to Earl and Emily on the occasion of their 71st wedding anniversary in 1983. (Courtesy of the author)

The Citation was followed by another great honor when this writer contacted radio personality Paul Harvey regarding Earl and Emily's marital milestone. Harvey subsequently announced the occasion of their 71st wedding anniversary to the world:

"Emily and Earl Dane Kidder, of Milton, Wisconsin, are celebrating seventy-one years…on their way to forever together."

Newspapers from three surrounding cities, including Janesville, the county seat, ran lengthy articles on their lives with emphasis on their marital milestone.

Earl became very ill in the fall of 1986 and developed a very severe infection in the artificial hip that doctors put in decades earlier after it was crushed in a farm accident. During his stay at Edgerton Hospital he repeatedly asked to see Emily, his beloved wife of nearly three quarters of a century.

With the help of family members, Emily, who was very fragile herself, was taken for a surprise visit to see Earl. As she was wheeled into Earl's hospital room, Earl's eyes filled with tears. He was unable to speak. Emily

Earl and Emily celebrate their 73rd wedding anniversary at their Milton farmhouse in 1985, surrounded by their five surviving children. From left: Warren, Bernice, Marian, Mildred, and Earl, Jr., "Bub." (Courtesy of the author)

Earl and Emily share one last kiss at the Edgerton Hospital.
(Top/Bottom—Courtesy of the author)

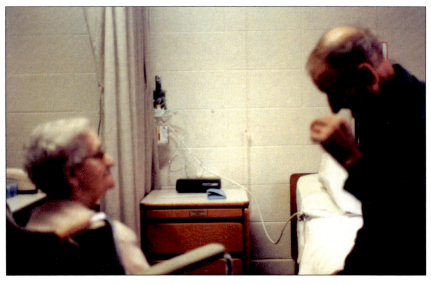

Earl wipes away the tears after sharing what would be his last kiss with Emily.

recognized him immediately. "Hi, Earl," she said, in a barely audible voice. She reached out to him, and he to her. Earl then leaned forward and gave her a kiss. He knew deep in his heart that it would be their last. Doctors soon operated, but at age ninety-three, Earl did not have the strength he needed to recover. He passed away around noon on August 14th, 1986. He was ninety-three years old.

In her final months Emily's mind nearly ceased to function, but there were two things that clung to the last vestiges of her memory. She would sit in her little maple rocking chair in the living room of their Milton farmhouse and sing, word for word, the hymns she once performed over seventy years earlier at the little church at Sandy Sink—"Jesus Loves Me," "The Little Brown Church in the Vale," "Just As I Am," and "Onward Christian Soldiers."

She would pause occasionally and ask where Earl was. They had never been separated for more than two weeks in their nearly seventy-five years together. Family members would tell her of Earl's passing, but she would forget what she was told just moments later. Although her mind would not enable her to remember Earl's death, it appeared that deep in her heart she knew, for it was just thirteen weeks after Earl's passing when this writer looked in on her around midnight on November 21st, 1986 and found that she had passed away peacefully in her sleep. She was ninety-four years old.

On the dresser next to her bed lay the little brass pin that held the photo of her father—the cherished possession that she

The little brass pin containing a photo of Emily's father, which Emily carried with her on the orphan train, and kept close to her for over eight decades. (Courtesy of the author)

carried with her on the orphan train. She had kept it close to her, treasuring it, for over eight decades.

Emily's long journey was over. She somehow managed to find the strength to persevere in a life that was filled with overwhelming adversity. She had met a plethora of seemingly insurmountable challenges head on and ultimately, against all odds, the little abandoned girl from Brooklyn managed to live the American dream.

Emily was laid to rest beside Earl and their son Don in the Milton East Cemetery. A large heart is etched in the center of their gray granite monument. Inside the heart are the words *"Married 74 Years."*

One can't help think, as Paul Harvey did, that they will always be "forever together."

APPENDIX I

THE REST OF THE STORY

The information below reveals what happened to the other children who accompanied Emily when she left New York on the orphan train, as well as what became of some of the people and places that touched Earl and Emily's lives. Reverend Clarke's journals were the source for the information on the children that appears in quotes, except where otherwise noted.

Alfred Baumann—Reverend Clarke: "Alfred Baumann was born February 13th, 1903. He was one of the finest boys. He had been deserted by his parents, or relatives. Matt Pierce took him, and about worshipped him, as did his [Matt's] daughter, Kittie. Alfred often wrote me after that, up until about 1913, when I heard nothing more."

The following information was given to this writer by Alfred's daughter, Joan Drahos:

Alfred Baumann

"The Pierce family never adopted Alfred, but he did adopt their last name. He married Clara Anna Augusta Gienapp, a native of Hopkinton [Iowa], on May 30, 1926. Both had attended

Lenox College in Hopkinton. Alfred later owned a grocery store, and worked in shipyards in California, and Wisconsin. He became a teacher in Center Point, Iowa, where he was voted the most popular citizen in a poll conducted by the local newspaper in 1937. Later, he became school principal in La Porte City, Iowa, and spent more than 25 years working with Boy Scouts. He received the 'Silver Beaver' award from the Scouts, which was their highest scouting award. He and his wife had two children; Alfred, Jr., and Joan Marilyn. They produced nine grandchildren, who in turn produced 14 great-grandchildren. Alfred, Sr., became an appraiser later in life, and died May 1, 1975, in Wautoma, Wisconsin, at age 72."

Joan added that her father, "believed in talking to youngsters instead of physical punishment. She added, "I only had one spanking in my young years—and I was no angel!"

Kathleen Marie Belt—Reverend Clarke: "Kathleen Belt was destined to be a great sufferer. She was born September 29th, 1896. A young man in her first home disliked her, and she was removed. The second home had no children, and her faults were greatly magnified, and told over and over at the tables in front of her, and in front of company at the house. I took her to Missouri. Here, she was bewitched, and her foster parents did not know how to manage her, and the poor thing had to go. All these homes had good references, but failed to keep her. I brought her to Minnesota. She would go to school with bleeding lips, or cheeks, or arm, or something, and would tell that her foster mother did it when punishing her. At last she fell down stairs, and broke her arm. The doctors declared the arm was not broken, but it became stiff at the elbow, and her flesh as hard as a bone. I visited her, and asked if she had been punished severely, and she said 'No.'

Kathleen Belt

One cold winter evening the home burned down, and she had to be taken to a neighbor. She was then returned to me again. Our Ladies Aid Society of the church clothed her up again, and she stole a few cents while they were doing it for her. She bought bananas with the money, and treated the women before it was discovered. I took her to the New York City Hospital for treatment, and then she was removed to another home. I visited her, finding her in a most pitiable condition. The poor child would weep for me to help her. At last she died of rheumatism about the heart. Why must a child suffer like that?"

Amy Calhoun—Reverend Clarke: "Amy was born January 17th, 1898. She was a bright Irish girl, and was taken by a jeweler, adopted, and well educated. I hear nothing from her now, but I always called on her when in that vicinity."

Further research reveals that Pharmacist Walter Doan and his wife—a childless couple—had selected Amy. She graduated from high school in 1917. Amy was given musical training and became a fine pianist. She attended Lenox College in Hopkinton, Iowa.[1]

Amy Calhoun

Bernice Lindergren with her foster parents.

Bernice Lindergren—The Ben Ferguson family of Hopkinton, Iowa adopted Bernice. Reverend Clarke: "Bernice was a baby of the party, and a sweet one she was. She was born December 25th, 1905. She was adopted, but later on her foster mother died. The 'grandmother' cared for her, along with her foster father, and she has been in school doing well. She sends me an occasional word. She grew up to be a nice young lady."

Samuel Orr—Nothing is recorded about him.

Gertrude Perry—Reverend Clarke: "Gertrude was born September 24th, 1901. She was a bright and active child, and was very small for her age. She had three homes before she was settled permanently. She was very nervous, but had promise. She liked music, and was a pianist. She finally went to Lansing, Iowa, up on the Mississippi Bluffs, with Seventh Day Adventists, and wrote me nice letters. She went to music school in Indiana.

Samuel Orr

Gertrude Perry

Relatives that were found at Albany, New York wanted me to give her money to visit them, but I refused, thinking I had to ask some questions regarding them first. This made her angry. She went, and was never heard from again."

Ira and Joseph Rowland—Reverend Clarke: "Ira Rowland was born June 29th, 1900. Joseph was born February 17th, 1903. Ira went to a French family, and Joseph to a German family. The German family had three daughters of peculiar makeup. One had black eyes, and brown hair. The other had brown eyes, and black hair. The third had pink eyes, and white hair (albino)."

Joseph was adopted by the Karth family of Hopkinton, Iowa. They were German

Ira (right) and Joseph (left) Rowland

farmers. He later left the family when he was of age and returned to New York. He was never heard from again. A. D. Leclere, a farmer, took Ira. He later returned to New York, and became a diving bell worker.[2]

PEOPLE AND PLACES THAT TOUCHED EARL & EMILY'S LIVES

Reverend Herman D. Clarke—Herman Devillo Clarke was born in Plainfield, New York on November 26th, 1850. He was the only child born to Nelson and Maria (Jennings) Clarke. When a young man he was blinded in his left eye when a nail he was hammering while repairing a chicken coop at his parent's farm was propelled into it. Herman was later educated at De Ruyter Institute, Winfield Academy, and Alfred University, in New York. He studied music at Lyons Musical Academy as well, being a pupil of L. H. Sherwood, father of William H. Sherwood, who was for a time America's most famous pianist.

Herman was strongly inclined to make music his profession and was the author of several books and many songs, both sacred and sentimental. He decided early in life that his duty was to preach the gospel after spending four summers (1879-1882) in gospel tent work with a Seventh Day Baptist minister named Reverend L. C. Rogers. Clarke took the pastorate of the First and Second Seventh Day Baptist Churches at Verona, New York in 1882, and was ordained on November 3rd, 1883. He later held pastorates in Independence, New York; Dodge Center, Minnesota; and Garwin, Iowa.

On September 17th, 1874, he married Miss Anna M. Jennings. They had three children; Mabel, who became Mrs. Charles Sayre; Florence, who became Mrs. Arthur Ellis; and Elvan H. Clarke.

It was while he was at Dodge Center, Minnesota that Herman became greatly interested in the work of the New York Children's Aid Society. He was asked to serve on a local committee that was established by Mr.

E. Trott, a placing agent working on behalf of the Society, just prior to the arrival of a group of children on May 24, 1898. The committee was to screen potential foster families. He became more and more interested in the work over time, and by 1900 he became a full-time placing and visiting agent for the Children's Aid Society.

Anna Laura Hill—The placing agent who accompanied Emily and the other children on the orphan train. Anna was born in Burlington, Pennsylvania on November 17, 1878. She was a graduate of the Mansfield Normal School. She moved to Elmira, New York when a young girl, and was a school teacher prior to her employment at the Children's Aid Society, which she began in 1902. Anna spent her last days in Elmira, New York at 1525 W. Water Street. She never married.

Anna Laura Hill as an older woman. (Courtesy of Mary Ellen Johnson)

Miss Hill died August 17, 1962 at the age of eighty-four. She had devoted thirty years of her life to the Children's Aid Society, retiring in 1932. She maintained contact with many of the children until they reached maturity, just as Reverend Clarke had. She was remembered fondly by many of them. She would often remember their birthdays with various gifts.

Miss Hill was held in special regard by two twin girls named Nettie and Nellie Crook who were sent on an orphan train to Kansas in 1911. Miss Hill accompanied them, and when it appeared that they were to be split up at the distribution, she insisted that they be kept together. She stayed in touch with the girls over the years and sent them each wedding presents. This speaks volumes about the character of Anna Laura Hill. Anna is buried in Woodlawn Cemetery in Elmira, New York.[3]

Mamie Gunderson—Emily's fellow ward at The Home for Destitute Children. Reverend Clarke recorded:

> "One most interesting case was that of Miss Mamie Gunderson of Rockport (sic) [Missouri]. She was on a farm and a member of the family was a President or Professor of a College somewhere in Missouri. This girl was an excellent scholar and was hungry for a higher education. She wanted me to give her such an opportunity and with the consent of her foster parents I took her to one of our Seventh Day Baptist College towns [Milton, Wisconsin], and sent her through high school. She graduated at the head of her class. She had worked for her board by caring for two 'feeble-minded' children.
>
> "She was a most beautiful young woman and very winning—a strong, healthy, and hard working one. In 1913, when I was Superintendent of the Haskell Home at Battle Creek, Michigan, I made her Assistant Matron and she was most excellent help, kind and patient with the children and never grumbled over extra work. She endeared herself to all by her winning ways and lovely disposition. She returned to Milton and completed her course. In the summer of 1914, she returned to Battle Creek for employment in the Sanitarium, and in the fall she entered Milton College with a scholarship. She had bright prospects intellectually, but had a hard struggle financially. She had refused an offer of marriage and began to keep company with another young man who seemed to worship the ground she walked on, but he was not worthy of her and I cautioned her not to give him encouragement unless she 'meant business.' She broke it off."

The following information was provided by Mamie's son, Charles Rose:

"Mamie, at the age of eleven, along with two of her younger brothers, was taken on an orphan train to Rock Port, Missouri, on January 19, 1905. Her foster parents did not live up to their contract in regards to sending her to high school. She desperately wanted to go, so she had written Reverend Clarke. He had many Seventh Day Baptist friends in Wisconsin, and knew of a couple named North that needed help caring for two "feeble-minded children."

It was ironic that Mamie and Emily had both been in the Home for Destitute Children and both ended up in Milton, Wisconsin. Mamie arrived in July 1910, just under a year after Reverend Clarke had brought Emily there. Mamie was then 14 years old. There is no evidence to suggest that she and Emily knew of each other during Mamie's stay in Milton.

In 1975, at the age of 81, Mamie recorded her life story on thirty pages of a notebook, including her memories of her stay at the Home for Destitute Children. Mamie died in Junction City, Kansas, on March 10, 1990 at the advanced age of ninety-seven years and nine months.

Emily's Birthplace—This writer made a trip to Brooklyn, New York in October of 1999 to visit the birthplace of my grandmother, Emily, with the hope that the building was still standing. A good friend of this writer, Mr. Jeremey Stuart De Fischberg, offered to drive my wife and I to the location. We crossed an old bridge that connected Manhattan and Brooklyn with potholes so large that I thought for sure Jeremey's little car would be swallowed up by one of them.

As we made our way up Myrtle Avenue we passed one of the addresses where Emily's parents once lived, but found that the buildings no longer existed. As we made our way another block towards the address where Grandma was born I spied a little group of storefronts that was still standing to our left in the shadows of a partially dismantled elevated railroad. There, on the front of one of the buildings, were the numbers "1333." It was an amazing experience to stand in front of the building where my grandmother was born some 107 years earlier. I'll not soon forget the excitement I felt that day.

The front of the building was covered with graffiti, and though I would have liked to examine the interior of the building, it was located in a very questionable neighborhood. The rather threatening stares of one of the occupants from an upstairs window convinced us we needed to be on our way. I snapped a few photos and we left.

The Home for Destitute Children—School No. 3 (part of the Brooklyn Industrial School Association)—The Home that Emily and her brother Richard were placed in at 217 Sterling Place, between Flatbush and Vanderbilt Avenues in Brooklyn, has since been demolished. The Home was built in 1862, with additional wings added in 1880 and 1890. In 1921, The Brooklyn Industrial School Association, Eastern District and Home for Destitute Children had its name legally changed to the Brooklyn Home For Children. They were legally merged in November 1927 by court order. The Home on Sterling place was subsequently sold to the Brooklyn Foundation in December 1929 for $375,000. The 100th Anniversary of the original Home was celebrated in 1954. The Brooklyn Home for Children exists today as Forestdale, Inc. in Forest Hills, New York.[4]

The Elizabeth Home for Girls as it looked in 2008. (Courtesy of Christopher Gray)

The Elizabeth Home for Girls—The "Reform School" for girls that Emily transferred to from the Home for Destitute Children still stands to this day. It was the subject of an article in the New York Times on June 8, 2008 by Christopher Gray. A photo of Emily ran with the article, as well as a brief synopsis of her life and connection with the Home. The article tells of how the Florence Critenton League occupied the building in the 1960s and '70s, and assisted with troubled young women, and that the interior of the building was stripped in a 1982 co-op conversion.

United Charities Building—The building where Emily and the other children gathered prior to their journey on the orphan train still stands at 105 East 22nd Street in New York City. It is now a National Historic Landmark, but is not open to the public.

Union Station—The Chicago railroad terminal where Emily and the others in the company arrived before being transferred to a different train at the Chicago and Northwestern terminal for the remainder of their trip to Hopkinton, Iowa, was demolished in 1925 to make way for additional tracks entering the concourse of the new Union Station, which was erected a block to the south.

Sandy Sink Church—The country church that Earl and Emily attended was purchased by a gentleman in 1922 for $250.00 after it had ceased to be used as a church. Before the new owner was able to use the building it was struck by lightning and burned to the ground. Years later the old fieldstones that formed its foundation were used as fill when nearby County Road H was improved and renamed Highway 51.

On the occasion of my grandparents' 71st wedding anniversary I wanted to give them something special, so I began a hunt for a photograph of the church that had been such an integral part of their young lives. I was fortunate enough to locate what may be the only surviving photo of the church. It belonged to a family who lived nearby whose ancestor helped build the church in 1870. I presented an 8 x 10 framed photo to Grandma and Grandpa on their special day. Though Grandma was unable to recognize the old building in the photo, Grandpa knew what it was immediately.

I'd never even seen his eyes well up with tears before, but they did that day. He placed the photo on the little buffet that stood on the wall between their bedrooms. Each night, as he headed to bed to retire for the evening, he would stop at the buffet, pick up the photo, and after studying it for a few moments, he would lovingly put it back in its place.

The Granary Home—The old granary that Earl and Emily renovated into a home, and which was later occupied by Earl's brother Clark and his wife Eunice. It was moved behind Earl's boyhood home, which still stands on Kidder Road. The granary was being used as a garage and storage shed, but has recently been razed.

The Ayreshire Stock Farm—The farm home where Earl and Emily reared their children on Kidder Road still stands, as well as the nearby barn that Earl built.

The Cottages—The stone and wood cottages that Earl built on the Ken Parker estate are still standing. The two stone cottages were later joined together, creating one large one.

Earl and Emily's Final Home—The farm that Earl and Emily spent their final years in on County N in Milton Township was sold in 2002. The new owners decided not to restore the farmhouse, and it was burned down as a training exercise for the Milton Fire Department in 2003. They did restore the century-old barn that stood just west of the house and the land was restored to a prairie.

Emily's Mother, Laura Amelia (Scott) Reese—The fate of Emily's mother is unknown. A granddaughter remembered traveling with her father, Lewis Reese, Jr., when a young girl. As they drove by either the city of Kingston or Blauvelt, New York, her father commented that his mother was buried there. This author has tried to no avail to locate her burial record or grave. She was last found on the 1900 U.S. Census under the name Amelia Reese. She was a boarder in the home of a family in Brooklyn and her occupation was listed as "nurse."

Earl and Emily's Children—Mildred, the oldest, went to college at the Normal School in Whitewater, Wisconsin and came back to teach in the local one-room schools of Oakdale, North Milton, and Kidder. She herself had attended the Oakdale school through eighth grade. It was at Oakdale that she taught her sister, Marian, as well as her brother, Warren. She married Walter Yahnke and later went on to become Superintendent of Schools in Rock County. One of her favorite stories to relate was how one of her high school classmates used to offer his entire lunch in trade for just one of her mother's homemade dill pickles, made from the same recipe as the pickle that Emily had snuck into Earl when he was recovering from pneumonia so many years earlier.

Bernice married Clair Punsel and they lived in the city of Janesville. She was a great help to her parents in their later life. They adopted a daughter, Susan.

Earl, Jr. "Bub" married Louise Maas and together they operated the family farm on Kidder Road. They had one son, James.

Warren followed in his father's footsteps and became a Constable for Milton and Fulton Townships. He was later made Chief of Police for Milton Township, as well as Captain of the Rock River Safety Patrol. He served fifty-three years as a police officer and over thirty years on the boat patrol, saving many lives on the choppy waters of nearby Lake Koshkonong. He served many years on the Rock County Parks Commission, and operated the 174-acre farm in Milton Township along with his parents. He married Nancy Olmstead. These were the writer's parents. They also had another son, Ronald.

Marian married Donald Boughton who later became one of Janesville's first chiropractors. They reside near Janesville, Wisconsin. They had four children, Douglas, Daniel, Jane, and Bradley.

Emily's Brother, Richard—This writer began a search for my grandmother Emily's brother, Richard Reese, several years ago. I did a search in the Social Security Death Index for every man with the first name of Richard born on February 8, 1890 in Brooklyn, New York. I then ordered the application papers for the six or seven individuals who turned up. I knew Richard served in the Army and this narrowed the field down to one. This particular gentleman was a resident of Baltimore, Maryland at the time he applied for Social Security. His name was Richard MacKay.

I placed several queries on various genealogy websites under the surname MacKay. Within a few months I received an e-mail from a person identifying themselves as a cousin of Richard MacKay's. He was able to confirm that *their* Richard had been adopted. I still wasn't entirely sure that I had the right person. I then ordered Richard MacKay's personnel file from the National Archives, which gave a detailed history of his employment from a teenager on up to his employment with U. S. Customs, and finally, his seat on the U. S. Railroad Retirement Board. The papers confirmed that Richard was small in stature, being very close to Emily's height of four feet ten inches, which seemed to suggest I had the right person.

It wasn't until later that another adoptive cousin of Richard's was able to provide proof that Richard MacKay was indeed one and the same as my great uncle and Emily's brother, Richard Reese. Proof came in the form of a series of photos. Richard's cousin graciously gave me

Richard (Reese) Mackay, October 1, 1944
Baltimore, MD
(Courtesy of Linda Smith)

several originals from her album and provided me with much insight into the life and personality traits of Richard. Richard married Marguerite Hood and had a stepdaughter named Lillian. He died in Baltimore, Maryland in 1969. I do so regret that he and my grandmother were never reunited.

APPENDIX II

END NOTES

Chapter 1

1. "During the last twenty years, a tide of population has settled towards those shores, to which there is no movement parallel in history. During the year 1852 alone, 300,992 alien passengers have landed in New York, or nearly at the rate of *one thousand a day for every week day.*" Children's Aid Society, First Annual Report (1854), 3-4.

2. John William Leonard, *History of the City of New York 1609-1909* (New York: Journal of Commerce and Commercial Bulletin, 1910), 539. According to Leonard, "The population of New York City in 1850 was, by Federal census, 515,477, and in 1860, 805,658." The 10,000 figure is given in Children's Aid Society, First Annual Report (New York, 1854), 4.

3. George W. Matsell, chief of police in the New York City Police Department, *Semi-Annual Report*, May 31-October 31, 1849 (New York, 1849), Appendix. This is from an excerpt in Robert H. Bremner, ed., *Children & Youth in America, vol. 1* (Cambridge, Mass.: Harvard Univ. Press, 1972), 755.

4. Children's Aid Society, *First Annual Report* (1854), 5.

5. David J. Rothman, "Our Brothers' Keepers," *American Heritage* 24 (December 1972): 42. The quote is from a "committee conducting a statewide survey in New York" in 1857.

6. Website titled *Department of Juvenile Justice,* located at www.nyc.gov/html/djj/html/1861.html

7. Andrea Warren, *Orphan Train Rider—One Boy's True Story,* (Boston: Houghton Mifflin Company, 1996), 17.

8. Edward K. Spann, *The New Metropolis: New York City, 1850-1857* (New York: Columbia University Press, 1981), 262.

Chapter 2

1. Marilyn Irvin Holt, *The Orphan Trains.* (Lincoln, Nebraska: University of Nebraska Press, 1992), 41.

2. Ibid., 44.

3. Ibid., 45.

4. Brace, *The Dangerous Classes*, 54-55.

5. Ibid., 78-9.

6. Quoted in Kristine Elisabeth Nelson, "The Best Asylum: Charles Loring Brace and Foster Family Care" (Ph.D. diss., University of California at Berkeley, 1980), 223.

7. Emma Brace, ed., *The Life of Charles Loring Brace Chiefly Told in His Own Letters* (New York: Scribner's Sons, 1894), 158.

8. Brace, *The Dangerous Classes,* 88-89.

9. Ibid., 92.

10. Clark Kidder, *Orphan Trains and Their Precious Cargo*, (Bowie, Maryland: Heritage Books, Inc., 2001), 10-11.

11. Children's Aid Society, *First Annual Report* (1854), 9.

12. E. P. Smith's journal, which was published in Charles Loring Brace, *Third Annual Report of the Children's Aid Society* (New York: M. B. Wynkoop, 1856), 54-60.

13. Leslie Wheeler, "The Orphan Trains," *American History Illustrated*, (December 1983): 10.

14. Children's Aid Society Annual Reports from the 1860s and 1870s.

15. Howard Zinn, *A People's History of the U.S.* (New York: Harper & Row, 1980), 235-238.

16. Wheeler, "The Orphan Trains," 21.

17. Holt, *The Orphan Trains*, 115.

18. *World-Herald* (Omaha, Neb.), December 15, 1921.

19. "Ship 90,000 babies from New York City," *The Janesville (WI) Daily Gazette*, Wednesday, December 20, 1899, Front page. The news wire originated in Chicago, Illinois.

20. Stephen O'Connor, *Orphan Trains: The Story of Charles Loring Brace and the Children He Saved and Failed*, (Boston—New York, Houghton Mifflin, 2001), 174.

21. Clark Kidder, *Orphan Trains and Their Precious Cargo*, 3.

22. John von Hartz, *New York Street Kids—136 Photographs Selected by The Children's Aid Society*, (New York: Dover Publications, Inc.), 39.

23. Quoted in *Children and Youth in America: A Documentary History*, 3 vols., edited by Robert H. Bremner et al. (Cambridge, Mass.: Harvard University Press, 1970-74), 2:365.

24. Ibid., 2:366-67.

25. O'Connor, Ibid. 308. From information in the archives of the Children's Aid Society.

26. Ibid., 256.

Chapter 3

1. Birth record No. 3467, on file at Municipal Archives in New York City. Date of return was April 1, 1893.

2. *Brooklyn (NY) Eagle*, August 8, 1898: 12.

3. *The Centennial of the Brooklyn Home For Children 1854-1954*, (November 1954). Pages not numbered.

4. *Forty-Sixth Annual Report of the Board of Managers of the Brooklyn Industrial School Association and Home For Destitute Children*, (Brooklyn: Eagle Press, 1900).

5. *New York Times*, June 8, 2008; article on the Home by Christopher Gray.

Chapter 4

1. Wheeler, "The Orphan Trains," 20.

2. Ibid., 20.

3. Brace, *The Dangerous Classes*, Ibid, 307.

4. Clark Kidder, *Orphan Trains and Their Precious Cargo*, 28.

5. Ibid., (p. 19).

6. Journals of Rev. H. D. Clarke.

7. Clark Kidder, *Orphan Trains and Their Precious Cargo*, 19.

8. The Janesville Gazette, Ibid.

9. Weather conditions for the day of their arrival were obtained from the *Chicago Daily News*.

10. Clark Kidder, *Orphan Trains and Their Precious Cargo*, 133.

11. Andrea Warren, *We Rode the Orphan Trains*, (Boston: Houghton Mifflin, 2001), 36.

12. Ibid., 19.

13. Wheeler, "The Orphan Trains," 18.

14. Quoted in *Children and Youth in America: A Documentary History*, 3 vols. Ibid., 2:307.

15. Clark Kidder, *Orphan Trains and Their Precious Cargo*, 8.

16. Ibid., 24.

17. Ibid., 73.

18. Ibid., 7.

19. The Janesville Daily Gazette, Ibid.

20. Clark Kidder, *Orphan Trains and Their Precious Cargo*, 233.

21. Miriam Z. Langsam, *Children West: A History of the Placing-Out System of the New York Children's Aid Society, 1853-1890* (Madison: State Historical Society for the Department of History, University of Wisconsin, 1964), 56.

22. Kristine Elisabeth Nelson, "The Best Asylum," 236.

Chapter 5

1. David & Elizabeth Metzger Armstrong, *The Great American Medicine Show*, (New York—London: Prentice Hall, 1991), 177.

2. Appears in *Brule County (SD) History* (Brule County Historical Society), 11-13. No date, but post-1974. The information is taken from an unidentified earlier publication.

3. *Inventory of the Church Archives of Wisconsin—Church of the United Brethren In Christ*; prepared by The Wisconsin Historical Records Survey Project, Division of Professional and Service Projects, Works Projects Administration; Madison, Wisconsin; April 1940, Record No. 123.

Chapter 7

1. O'Connor, *Orphan Trains*, 309. Kansas and Missouri also claim the dubious honor of having received the last orphan train.

Appendix I

1. A typewritten letter on file at the Orphan Train Heritage Society of America from Earl H. DeShaw, M. D., Physician and Surgeon, Monticello, Iowa. No date.

2. Ibid.

3. *The Chemung Historical Journal*, Vol. 36, No. 2, Elmira, New York, (December 1990), 4005.

4. *The Centennial of the Brooklyn Home For Children,* Ibid.

APPENDIX III

SOURCES FOR RECORDS ON ORPHAN TRAIN RIDERS

Primary Sources

Brooklyn Nursery and Infant's Hospital
c/o Salvation Army
Foster Home and Adoption Services
233 East 17th Street
New York, NY 10003

Children's Aid Society
Office of Closed Records
150 East 45th Street
New York, NY 10017

Children's Home of Cincinnati—Founded in 1864
5050 Madison Road
Cincinnati, OH 45227
PH: 513-272-2800

Home for the Friendless
(Established by The American Female Guardian Society—Founded in 1834)
Records are being indexed by:
The Orphan Train Heritage Society of America,
614 E. Emma Avenue, Suite 115, Springdale, AR 72764-4634

New York Juvenile Asylum—Founded in 1851
c/o Children's Village
Office of Alumni Affairs
Dobbs Ferry, NY 10522

Five Points House of Industry
c/o Greer-Woodycrest and Hope Farm
Mr. Mark Lukens, Director
Crystal Run Village
RD 2, Box 98
Middletown, NY 10940

Brooklyn Home for Children—Since 1921
(formerly The Home for Destitute Children—Founded in 1854)
c/o Forestdale, Inc.
67-35 112th Street
Forest Hills, NY 11375-2349
Open Monday through Friday (9-5 p.m.)

New England Home for Little Wanderers
850 Boylston Street, Suite 201
Chestnut Hill, MA 02167
On the web: www.thehome.org

New York Child's Foster Home Services
(for Sheltering Arms and Speedwell records)
c/o Sheltering Arms
122 East 29th Street
New York, NY 10016

New York Infant Asylum
(merged in 1910 with New York Nursery and Child's Hospital)
c/o Mrs. Adele Lerner
Medical Archives
New York Hospital Cornell Medical Center
1300 York Avenue
New York, NY 10021

National Orphan Train Complex
P. O. Box 322
300 Washington Street
Concordia, KS 66901
Phone/Fax: (785)-243-4471
Website: www.orphantraindepot.org
(Publishes a quarterly and has documented information on over 10,000 riders; sponsors orphan train rider reunions)

New York Foundling Hospital
(Name changed from New York Foundling Asylum in the 1890s—Founded in 1869)
Department of Closed Records
590 Avenue of the Americas
New York, NY 10011-2019
PH: 718-596-5555

The Orphan Asylum Society of Brooklyn—Founded in 1832
c/o Brookwood Child Care (1960—present)
25 Washington
Brooklyn, NY 11201
(Have records back to 1855)

Original records were sent to:
University of Minnesota—Social Welfare History Archives
101 Walter Library
117 Pleasant Street, S. E.
Minneapolis, MN 55455
http://special.lib.umn.edu/swha

The Orphan Asylum Society of New York City
c/o Graham-Windham Services to Families and Children
One South Broadway
Hastings-on-Hudson, NY 10706

Sources On the Web

Cyndi's List
Lists numerous websites related to orphan train research.
http://www.cyndislist.com/orphans.htm#Orphans

Legends & Legacies: Orphanages
Browse the growing list of known orphanages nationally and internationally, plus learn about the history and types of orphanages.
http://www.legends.ca/orphanages/orphanages.html

Orphan Train—A Wisconsin GenWeb Project
Collects information and photos of Wisconsin Orphan Train Riders. Author Clark Kidder is the official researcher for the site, and has contributed much of the information and photographs.
http://www.rootsweb.com/~wiorphan

Orphan Train Riders History
Howard Hunt recounts his childhood as a 3-year-old orphan train rider with his 6-year-old brother in upstate New York, 1925.
http://www.hamilton.net/subscribers/hurd/index.html

Orphan Trains of Iowa—An IA GenWeb Special Project
Extensive photographs and records on Iowa orphan train riders.
http://www.iagenweb.org/iaorphans/

Orphan Trains of Kansas
Search for the lost history and ancestry of orphan children sent from the streets of New York to the West between 1867 and 1930. A great site for Kansas orphan train research.
http://www.kancoll.org/articles/orphans/

Orphan Trains of Nebraska
Provides information on Nebraska orphan train riders. Actual accounts of orphan train riders.
http://www.rootsweb.com/~neadoptn/Orphan.htm

Orphan Trains—The American Experience
PBS documentary examines the efforts of the Children's Aid Society to find rural homes for homeless city youths between 1850 and 1929.
http://www.pbs.org/wgbh/pages/amex/orphan/

They Rode the Orphan Trains

Provides information on Missouri orphan train riders.

http://www.rootsweb.com/~mogrundy/orphans.html

APPENDIX IV

BIBLIOGRAPHY

Nonfiction:

Brace, Charles Loring. *The Dangerous Classes of New York and Twenty Years' Work among Them.* New York: 1880. Reprint, New Jersey: Patterson Smith, 1967.

Fry, Annette. *The Orphan Trains.* New York: New Discovery Books, 1994.

Gordon, Linda. *The Great Arizona Orphan Abduction.* Cambridge: Harvard University Press, 1999.

Holt, Marilyn Irvin. *The Orphan Trains.* Lincoln, Nebraska: University of Nebraska Press, 1992.

Johnson, Mary Ellen, and Kay B. **Hall**. *Orphan Train Riders: Their Own Stories*, Volumes I-V. Baltimore, Md.: Gateway Press. Available from the Orphan Train Heritage Society of America.

Kidder, Clark. *Orphan Trains and Their Precious Cargo—The Life's Work of Rev. H. D. Clarke*: Bowie, Md: Heritage Books, Inc., 2001.

O'Connor, Stephen. *Orphan Trains: The Story of Charles Loring Brace and the Children He Saved and Failed.* Boston and New York: Houghton Mifflin, 2001.

Patrick, Michael, Evelyn **Sheets**, and Evelyn **Trickel**. *We Are a Part of History.* Santa Fe, New Mexico: Lightning Tree Press, 1990.

Riis, Jacob A. *How the Other Half Lives.* New York: Charles Scribner's Sons, 1890.

Seller, Maxine Schwartz. *Immigrant Women.* Philadelphia: Temple University Press, 1981.

Vogt, Martha Nelson, and Christina **Vogt**. *Searching for Home: Three Families from the Orphan Trains.* Grand Rapids, Michigan: Triumph Press, 1986.

Warren, Andrea. *Orphan Train Rider—One Boy's True Story.* Boston, Mass.; Houghton Mifflin Company, 1996. An American Library Association Notable Book. Winner of the 1996 Boston Globe—Horn Book Award for Outstanding Nonfiction.

Wendinger, Renee. *Extra! Extra! The Orphan Trains and Newsboys of New York.* Sleepy Eye, Minnesota: Legendary Publications, 2009.

Fiction:

De Vries, David. *Home at Last.* New York: Dell, 1990.

Holland, Isabelle. *The Journey Home.* New York: Scholastic, 1990.

Nixon, Joan Lowery. *The Orphan Train Quartet: A Family Apart, Caught in the Act, In the Face of Danger, A Place to Belong.* New York: Bantam Books, 1987-1990.

Peart, Jane. *Orphan Train West Trilogy: Homeward the Seeking Heart, Quest for Lasting Love, Dreams of a Longing Heart.* Tarrytown, New York: Fleming H. Revell Co., 1990.

Petrie, Dorothea G., and James Magnuson. *Orphan Train.* New York: Dial Press, 1978.

Talbot, Charlene Joy. *An Orphan for Nebraska.* New York: Atheneum, 1979.

Magazine Articles:

American Heritage. "The Children's Migration"; Annette Riley Fry, Vol. XXVI, Number 1, December 1974, pages 4-10, 79-81.

American History Illustrated. "The Orphan Trains"; Leslie Wheeler, December 1983, pages 10-23.

The Goldfinch, Iowa History for Young People. Vol. 21, Number 3, Spring 2000.

Smithsonian. "It Took Trains to put Street Kids on the Right Track Out of the Slums"; Donald Dale Jackson, August 1986, pages 95-103.

The Palimpsest. "The Orphan Train Comes to Clarion"; Verlene McCollough, Fall 1988, pages 144-150.

Wisconsin Magazine of History. "West by Orphan Train"; Clark Kidder, Winter 2003-2004; pages 30-39.

Appendix V

Teacher Guide

Exercises, Academic Projects, and Tasks Incorporating the Reading of

Emily's Story

The Brave Journey of an Orphan Train Rider

By Clark Kidder

- In the Secondary & Postsecondary Classroom
- For Independent Study
- With Book Clubs

I. LESSON PLAN OPPORTUNITIES

A. Activities

1. Conduct an essay contest to pen stories about a grandparent or other older relative who has had a positive impact on the student's life. Author Clark Kidder is available to serve as the judge for such a contest. Contact him via e-mail at cokidder@hotmail.com. The curator of a local or county historical society, as well as an orphan train rider or a descendant of one, would also be candidates to serve as a judge.

2. Create trading cards that depict an orphan train rider, which could include those who rode the orphan train with Emily, or another that could be found in a book or on the Internet. Include the child's name, birth date (if known), the name of the institution they came from, the destination that the train was headed for, etc. The students could each give a short report about the rider they chose to "sponsor" for their particular card, or write a short fiction or nonfiction story about the rider's life.

3. Conduct a play based on the book. If a script is needed, the author, Clark Kidder, will provide one that he has written. In the event the students are old enough they could be encouraged to write their own script for a play. In lieu of a play, assign each child a line to read from the script provided with the PowerPoint Presentation that is available for purchase from author Clark Kidder. See ordering information at the end of this book. Present the play or PowerPoint reading to parents, other classes, local civic groups, etc.

4. Take turns reading selected passages aloud from the book.

5. Select one of the following characters from the book and discuss what else you would have liked to read about this person: Emily's mother,

Emily's father, Reverend H. D. Clarke, Anna Laura Hill, Emily's brother, Richard, or any other person in Emily's life. Taking what you know (or think you know; you can embellish), write a letter from that person to Emily.

6. If Emily had kept a diary, what would she have written in it during her stay at the orphanage, during her trip on the orphan train, during her stay at one of the foster homes, during her employment at the Sanitarium, after Earl's marriage proposal, after the death of one of her sons, or during her elderly years, as she looked back on her life? Pick a time period and enter your thoughts in the diary.

7. Arrange interviews with local orphan train riders, their descendants, or people knowledgeable about the orphan trains.

8. Make a diorama or model of what a train car might have looked like.

9. What would Emily have written in a letter to her parents during her stay at the orphanage or during her stay in one of the numerous foster homes? Pretend you are Emily and write such a letter.

10. Make flyers or posters advertising the coming of the orphan train to your hometown.

11. Draw a map showing the route Emily or another orphan train rider would have taken from New York City to the Midwest.

12. Make a graph showing the number of children placed in various states.

13. Interview a Human Services worker about homeless children and families in your particular county or state.

14. Create an Orphan Train Concept Chart divided into two columns that outline the pros and cons of placing out children via the orphan trains.

15. Divide children into groups that represent a potential foster family. Discuss or write the reasons why your family is desirous of an orphan train child, and what the child will be expected to do in regards to household duties, chores, etc.

16. Have each child write an orphan train poem. Themes may include the feelings you had when boarding the orphan train; fear of being sent to an unknown home; sadness, happiness, and other emotional feelings associated with being placed in an orphanage or being placed out. For some children the trip west was seen as an opportunity, but to others it meant heartbreak and disappointment.

17. Encourage the children to prepare (with a teacher or parent) one of the following recipes from Earl and Emily's cookbook:

Homemade Ice Cream

    6 Eggs
    4 cups of sugar
    3 Tablespoons of Corn Starch
    2 Quarts of milk
    1 Teaspoon salt
    2 Tablespoons Vanilla Extract
    2 Pints Whipping Cream
    2 Pints Half-and-Half
    1 or 2 bags of ice cubes

Mix the first 5 ingredients together in pan. Cook until it begins to boil and becomes quite thick. Cool. Add vanilla, whipping cream, and half and half. Freeze. Pack space surrounding freezer canister with ice, applied in layers, sprinkling salt on the ice as you slowly fill the freezer. (Earl and Emily often used icicles that had formed on the eaves of the house and farm buildings). Makes six quarts. The use of a manual ice cream maker (versus electric) would further duplicate the method used by Earl and Emily.

Molasses Popcorn Balls

2 cups of brown Karo Syrup

3 cups sugar

3-4 Tablespoons Molasses

1 Tablespoon butter

1 Tablespoon vinegar

One 2 lb. bag of popcorn to pop (approximately)

Mix the first five ingredients together in pan. Bring to a boil while stirring constantly. Boil until mixture reaches the "hair" stage. Hold the spoon above the pan and let a small amount of the mixture drip down into the pan. A very fine hair-like thread should form and curl back upwards toward the spoon in a wispy fashion. Add one teaspoon of vanilla and one half teaspoon of baking soda. Mixture will bubble up and turn a lighter color.

Pour mixture over lightly salted popcorn. Dip your hands in flour to form the popcorn balls. Leftover syrup can be used to make taffy. Butter your hands well before pulling the syrup into the size that you prefer. Taffy will lighten as it is pulled. Work quickly, as the syrup hardens fast. Cut into pieces while still somewhat soft.

B. Handout

1. How did Emily's interaction with her brothers and sisters impact her life?

2. How did meeting and marrying Earl impact Emily's life?

3. Describe the roles of geography, terrain, and weather in the shaping of Emily's story.

4. Was placing children on orphan trains a fair practice? Why or why not?

5. What other options could have been implemented instead of sending the children on orphan trains?

6. How would you have felt in the same situation? What would have been your greatest fear?

7. What would you like your adoptive family to be like? Would you have preferred a home in the city to one in the country?

II. RESOURCES AND RESEARCH ACTIVITIES FOR EDUCATORS & OTHERS

1. Study early railroad maps and early plat maps of the region identifying train routes taken by the orphan trains as well as residences of characters from the book.

2. Visit the Wisconsin Historical Society website to learn more about life in Wisconsin and Rock County during the Twentieth Century.

3. Visit New York historical societies and museums (online or in person) from the ancestral communities of Emily, Reverend Clarke, and Anna Laura Hill.

4. Encourage scholars to visit local, county, regional or state historical societies or museums online and in person with the objectives of discovering records of people that rode on the orphan trains.

5. Encourage students and/or scholars to undertake their own research and oral interviews of living orphan train riders in their state or local communities.

III. USEFUL WEBSITES
(IN ADDITION TO THOSE LISTED PREVIOUSLY):

1. State Historical Societies—http://web.syr.edu/~jryan/infopro/hs.html

2. Rock County (WI) Historical Society—http://www.rchs.us/

3. Wisconsin Historical Society—http://wisconsinhistoricalsociety.org/

4. Milton (WI) Historical Society—http://www.miltonhouse.org/

5. How to conduct oral interviews—http://www.indiana.edu/~cshm/techniques.html

6. Cyndi's List—http://www.cyndislist.com/orphans.htm#Orphans

7. Author's Website—http://www.ClarkKidder.com

APPENDIX VI

RESOURCES AVAILABLE FROM THE AUTHOR

- An electronic Microsoft Word file of the above Teacher Guide is available from the author Clark Kidder at cokidder@hotmail.com. The author is also available to appear in classrooms via satellite for interactive discussions with students. In addition, he is available to give book lectures to your group or organization. Contact the author at the e-mail above for details.

- A PowerPoint Presentation, which includes a script that corresponds to each photo in the presentation (taken from actual photos and text in the book), is available in the form of a CD from the author at the above e-mail address. A few bonus photos that did not make it in the book are also included as part of the PowerPoint Presentation, as is special audio of Paul Harvey announcing Earl and Emily's 71st Wedding Anniversary on his radio show and an interview with Emily. Cost is $25.00 postage paid (in the U.S.), or $40.00 postage paid for foreign countries.

- The Author would greatly enjoy hearing from you regarding any questions or comments on this book. He may be contacted via e-mail at cokidder@hotmail.com.

- Signed copies of this book can be purchased from the author by e-mailing him at cokidder@hotmail.com or from his website http://www.ClarkKidder.com.

- This book is available on Amazon Kindle.

The Children

They are idols of hearts and of households;
They are angels of God in disguise;
The sunlight still sleeps in their tresses;
His glory still gleams in their eyes;
These truants from home and from Heaven,
They have made me more manly and mild;
And I know now how Jesus could liken
The kingdom of God to a child.

—Dickens

Author's note: Charles Dickens visited the Five Points area of Lower Manhattan, New York in 1841. The poem above was likely inspired by the appalling conditions he observed. Of the Five Points, he later commented: "Debauchery has made the very houses prematurely old…all that is loathsome, drooping and decayed is here."

About the Author

Clark Kidder resides in Wisconsin. He is a freelance writer for international publications and has authored several books including *Marilyn Monroe UnCovers* (Quon Editions, 1994); *Marilyn Monroe—Cover To Cover* (Krause Publications, Inc., 1999); *Marilyn Monroe Collectibles* (HarperCollins, 1999); *Orphan Trains and Their Precious Cargo* (Heritage Books, Inc., 2001); *Marilyn Monroe Memorabilia* (Krause Publications, Inc., 2001); *Marilyn Monroe—Cover To Cover, 2nd Ed.* (Krause Publications, Inc., 2003), and *A Genealogy of the Wood Family*, (Family Tree Publishers, 2003). His magazine articles have appeared in *The Wisconsin Magazine of History*, and *Family Tree Magazine*. Kidder was the recipient of the Hesseltine Award in 2004 for his article titled *West by Orphan Train*, which appeared in the Winter 2003-2004 issue of the *Wisconsin Magazine of History*.

Clark Kidder in Dubuque, Iowa.
(Photo by Bill Case)

Kidder has been interviewed by numerous reporters for articles in such newspapers as the *Los Angeles Times* and the *Chicago Tribune*. He has appeared on *MSNBC, PAX,* and *WGN* television as well as numerous radio shows around the nation. Kidder was host of his own television show called *Book Talk* on *JATV* in Janesville, Wisconsin. In addition, he has provided consultation and photographs for documentaries and television shows produced by *CBS* and *October Films* in London, England. He has traced his Kidder roots back to 1320 in Maresfield, Sussex, England. He is past Vice President of the Milton Historical Society, which operates the Milton House Museum—a National Landmark located in Milton, Wisconsin. Kidder also lectures on Orphan Train history on behalf of the Wisconsin Humanities Council Speakers Bureau.